TOWN·AND·CITY·GUIDES

AA

EDINBURGH

TOWN·AND·CITY·GUIDES

The all-in-one guide to what goes on in and around the city

*Tourist information,
maps, walks, drives,
eating out, where to stay*

Produced by the Publishing Division of the Automobile Association

Cover: Edinburgh Castle

Title page: Entrance to the Scottish United Services Museum, Edinburgh Castle

Editor: Betty Sheldrick
Copy Editor: Gail Harada
Art Editor: Bob Johnson
Design Assistant: K A G Design
Picture researcher: Wyn Voysey
Original Photography: Douglas Corrance
Editorial Contributors: Jim Bowman (Edinburgh's Villages);
The Cadies (City Walks); Iain Crawford (Introduction, The Story
of Edinburgh, The Festival and the Arts, Famous Residents);
Albert Morris (The Royal Mile); Basil Skinner (Capital Buildings);
Gilbert Summers (City Centre: Places to Visit, Out of City: Places
to Visit)

Directory compiled by Pam Stagg

Day Drives prepared by the Home Routes Research and
Development Unit of the Automobile Association

Maps and plans produced by the Cartographic Department of the
Automobile Association. Atlas based on the Ordnance Survey
maps, reproduced with the permission of the controller of Her
Majesty's Stationery Office. Crown copyright reserved.

Filmset by Vantage Photosetting Co Ltd, Eastleigh and London,
England

Printed and bound by Graficromo SA, Spain

Produced and distributed in the United Kingdom by the
Publishing Division of the Automobile Association, Fanum
House, Basingstoke, Hampshire, RG21 2EA.

ISBN 0 86145 653 x
AA Reference 50720

CONTENTS

Introduction

Mound Place, with the Royal Mile skyline behind, towers above the lush greenery of Princes Street Gardens

Edinburgh has been compared to many cities. In the 18th century it was known as 'The Athens of the North' and its many-hilled townscape has led to its being compared to Rome of the seven hills. The truth is that Edinburgh is its own place, unique in its combination of setting and its three towns, medieval, Georgian and Victorian, and many villages, with the hills and the sea and the countryside always visible.

Whichever way you enter the city it is immediately impressive, the Castle on its high rock floating above the roofs and steeples, the turrets and towers of the Old Town jagged along the spur which falls from its battlements to the Palace of Holyroodhouse.

It is only later that you discover the ordered elegance of the complex of linked squares, crescents and streets which is the Georgian New Town, and Edinburgh is so prodigal of architectural riches that many visitors never see the solid domestic grandeur of Victorian Morningside, Grange and Newington at all.

The Pelican History of Art describes the New Town as 'the most extensive example of a romantic classical city in the world' and its air of prosperous serenity is part of the Edinburgh ethos and character.

The Georgian House, restored and furnished in period by the National Trust for Scotland, in the magnificent Adam-designed Charlotte Square, offers a chance to study how the merchants, lawyers and aristocrats lived when they moved from the teeming squalor of the high lands of the Old Town across the Nor' Loch which once lay at the Castle foot, in the last years of the 18th century.

The street that runs from the Castle esplanade to the royal Palace of Holyroodhouse at the foot of Edinburgh's domestic mountain, Arthur's Seat, is the heart of the Old Town—the Royal Mile.

Between the tall houses or 'lands' on

either side, narrow wynds and alleys like bones growing from a spine, lead steeply to the hidden delights of medieval Edinburgh.

Much of the Old Town has been restored and down these narrow lanes, there are examples, sometimes fragmentary, sometimes more complete, of 15th- and 16th-century architecture to be seen among the small restaurants, boutiques and renovated houses.

The steepness of the site means that there are roads like the Cowgate and even large open spaces like the Grassmarket almost secreted below the Royal Mile.

Edinburgh is a city of many levels and unexpected vistas. Down some of the these plunging wynds, you catch the steel glint of the North Sea in the Firth of Forth, through others loom the green slopes of the Pentland Hills.

The craggy, haphazard architecture of the Old Town and the smooth elegance of the New present a contrast unmatched in any other city in the world. The more modern parts straggle out southwards towards the hills and north to the shores of the River Forth in solid Victorian splendour or less enticing suburban sprawl but all marvellously punctuated by green spaces.

Edinburgh, for example, has 26 golf courses within her city boundaries and 80 within half an hour's drive. Beyond the city the scenery is as varied as hills and sea can make it.

The tight, contained urban quality of the different Edinburghs exists only a few minutes from the countryside. It is a grey tumbling city, tugged at by winds and illuminated by the ever-changing light, where the green life and the sea life and call of the hills are never far away.

About this Book

Edinburgh City Guide
designed to be the complete guide for tourist or resident,
contains the following sections.

Features
Written by local experts, these introductory articles cover
subjects of special importance in the city—its history,
architecture, famous residents, the villages within Edinburgh,
the Royal Mile and the Festival.

City Centre: Places to Visit
Here places of interest, listed alphabetically, are described in
detail. Each entry includes its street name, so it can easily be
located on the street plan on page 104. For opening times and
practical information refer to the Directory.

City Walks
Six walks, with step-by-step route directions, have been
carefully planned to take in the best of the city. The chief places
of interest along the way are described in the text.

Out of City: Places to Visit
An alphabetical selection of the most attractive and interesting
towns, villages and places to visit in the surrounding area. All
within an hour or so's drive. For opening times etc refer to the
relevant section of the Directory. Each entry has a grid
reference, so can be located on the maps on pages 98–101.

Day Drives
Two routes for exploring the countryside around the city,
including detailed route directions, a map and places of interest.

District Maps
Four pages of mapping at a scale of 4 miles to the inch, covering
the area around the city, extending approximately 35 miles from
the city centre.

Throughroute Map
This shows the motorways and main roads in and out of the city.

Edinburgh City Plan
Large-scale map of the City Centre, with a street index and
places of interest clearly shown.

Directory
Thirteen pages packed with useful information grouped into
sections (see page 106). All you need to know about where to eat
and stay, recreation, shops, sports and services, plus useful
addresses and opening times for all the places of interest
described in the book. A calendar of events lists the major
annual festivals, shows and sporting events month by month.

FEATURES

Edinburgh is Scotland's main brewing centre, and there is a wealth of interesting and historical bars in which to sample the product

The Story
of
Edinburgh

EDINBURGH CASTLE
Majestic on its ancient rock, Edinburgh Castle is an impressive sight for all seasons. Ghostly in the haze of a spring morning, dramatic in relief against an amber sunset, floodlit and alive with fireworks during the Tattoo, or enshrouded in a white cloak of snow — its haunting presence dominates the city

The story of Edinburgh begins with the Rock. It was formed between the mountains and the sea from the old volcanic caldera of the Lothian valley with its lava slides and basalt plugs choking the throats of the ancient volcanoes, shaped later into crags and valleys by the flows of the Ice Age.

This rock on which the Castle now towers over the heart of Edinburgh, commands the sea-gate to Scotland in the east and the march route north, trod by the Romans, Saxons and the English.

From earliest days on this rock, Dun Edin (named perhaps for Edwin, a victorious Northumbrian king in the 7th century, or maybe the Gaelic title for the 'fortress of the hill-slope'), inevitably there crouched a castle, a fortress guarding the most vulnerable approaches to Scotland.

For 1,300 years it has been a refuge and a defiance to invaders. In the 5th century the Picts called it by a gentler title, Mynyd Eidden — Maidens' or Virgins' Castle — because they kept their daughters there, away from the rabble.

Edinburgh owes its existence to the supposed invincibility of this fortress and today its oldest building stands on its rock 300ft above the main thoroughfare, Princes Street.

Although there is evidence of Iron Age settlements on and around Arthur's Seat, Edinburgh's domestic mountain at the foot of the Royal Mile, St Margaret's Chapel is the oldest still extant structure and its origins coincide happily with the emergence of Edinburgh as Scotland's capital. It was built by David I, sixth son of the saintly Queen Margaret, the Hungarian-born English princess who married Macbeth's conqueror, Malcolm Canmore, when he moved the Scottish capital from Dunfermline to Edinburgh in 1124.

Queen Margaret exercised a civilising influence on the Scottish court and its king and was largely responsible for the assimilation of the old Celtic Church into the Church of Rome. She was canonised by Pope Innocent IV in 1251 and this casket of stone, on the highest place on the Castle Rock, is her memorial.

In the 30 years before David came to the throne there had been six kings, but he replaced the turbulence and strife of those times with order and peace.

Educated in England and more Norman than Scots, David, a pious and orderly man, introduced the feudal system to Scotland, built a number of abbeys and founded the city of Edinburgh round the Castle Rock. At first his new capital was little more than a village but when he built the Abbey of the Holy Rood at the end of the basalt spur which runs like a wedge from the Castle to the foot of Arthur's Seat, he created two villages which eventually became a town and later a city.

Legend has it that the pious David, hunting on a Sunday (not perhaps as heinous a crime then as it would have seemed after the Reformation!) was attacked and unseated by a stag at Holyrood. His life was saved only by grasping at a cross that had suddenly

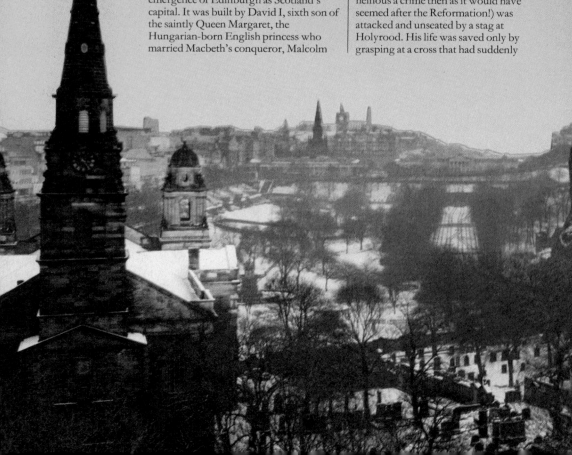

appeared between the stag's antlers and holding it up in a plea for Divine mercy. He founded the Abbey in gratitude for his delivery and an antlered stag with a cross on its forehead is still the coat of arms of the Canongate.

In 1633 Charles I was crowned there and its ruined walls still stand beside the royal Palace of Holyroodhouse. It survived in one form or another until the abdication of James VII in 1688 when the Protestant mob ravaged it on hearing of William of Orange's arrival in London.

FEUDS AND ASSASSINATION

The two burghs of Canongate and Edinburgh linked together gave Scotland a capital city and, after the fierce and bitter War of Independence under Robert the Bruce, in 1329 the victorious Scottish king granted a new charter to Edinburgh which established the city's rights over the Port of Leith.

The reigns of the early Stuarts, Bruce's successors as kings in the 15th century through his daughter, Marjory, were beset by feuds, battles and assassination and none of the first four Jameses died in bed.

The poetic James I was murdered in a tennis court in Perth. 'Fiery Face' James II was blown up by one of his great new cannons at Roxburgh Castle. The cultural dilettante, James III, was mysteriously murdered by a priest when fleeing from the Battle of Sauchieburn, and the flower of them all, the 'Renaissance Prince', James IV, died gallantly but uselessly on the field of Flodden.

Only James IV, who was 16, was other than a child when he came to the throne, and the whole history of the Stuarts up to James VI of Scotland and I of England is bedevilled by regencies and squabbles among ambitious and self-seeking guardians of the child monarchs.

When James IV came to the throne in 1488, Scotland seemed on the threshold of a new era. James had almost all the talents save one — discretion. He was handsome, accomplished in all the martial and social arts and a great many other things besides. He spoke eight languages, was skilled in medicine and gave Edinburgh a Royal College of Surgeons in 1506 and Scotland its first printing press in 1508. In 1496 he introduced the first compulsory Education Act.

High-spirited and lively, interested in everything from alchemy to music, he made Edinburgh into a city of European stature.

At the end of the Royal Mile, which leads down from the Castle to Holyrood, he built a splendid new palace to house his bride, the symbol of the union of the Thistle and the Rose, Margaret Tudor, daughter of Henry VII of England.

There had been a building of some kind beside Holyrood Abbey before, for James II was born there, but the royal residence had been in the Castle. Until James made it into a palace for his English Queen, Holyrood was probably a royal guest house, used when there were ceremonies at the Abbey.

EDENBVRG.

EDENBVRGVM. SCOTIAE METROPOLIS.

EDENBURGUM SCOTIAE METROPOLIS

An engraving of 16th-century Edinburgh showing the Old Town wall. Inset: James IV

But Queen Margaret's brother, Henry VIII, when he succeeded to the English throne, was not content to have peace along the Border. The marriage treaty with Scotland was broken by resumed Border raiding and what seemed to be a golden age in Scotland came to a tragic end.

Partly because of the renewal of Border strife and partly in response to a plea from the Queen of France for help against Henry, who had renewed the English claim to the throne of Louis XII by invading France, James assembled his army on the Boroughmuir (now the Meadows).

The Bore Stone set into the northern wall of Morningside Parish Church in Morningside Road is traditionally supposed to be that in which James set his standard before marching south into England and the greatest battle disaster in Scottish history.

At Flodden in the foothills of the Cheviots, in September 1513, James died with 10,000 of his men and 13 earls in a desperately fought but badly mismanaged conflict.

Once more the king of Scotland was a child. James V was two years old when his father died with the flower of Scottish chivalry at Flodden.

MOURNING AND TERROR

Edinburgh, in mourning and in terror, started work on a new wall around the city to defend it from invasion — fragments of a wall can still be seen, particularly in the Vennel on the western boundary of George Heriot's School and in Castle Wynd which leads from the Grassmarket up to the Castle Esplanade.

The feared invasion did not take place because Henry made his peace with France. By a supreme irony, typical of these devious times, when the instigator of the tragedy of Flodden, Queen Anne of France, died in 1514, her husband Louis XII married James IV's sister-in-law, Henry VIII's sister, Mary. The wedding celebrations with a bride of 16 proved too much for the 53-year-old French king and he dropped dead on 1 January 1515!

The affairs of Scotland and its child monarch were handled by an uneasy regency under Queen Margaret for a few months but she sacrificed her right to rule by remarrying. When she married the Earl of Angus, the new king's second cousin, the Duke of Albany, was summoned from France to be regent.

However, when he returned to France two years later to negotiate a treaty, he was held prisoner by the new French king, François I. Back in Edinburgh, the great families fought and squabbled for supremacy. The battle spilled out of the debating chambers into the streets of the capital. In 1520 it culminated in a bloody encounter between the Douglases and the Hamiltons up and down the Royal Mile and in and out of the wynds and vennels off it, which Edinburgh folk called 'The Cleansing of the Causeway.'

During this time the boy king was held prisoner in the Castle, but in 1528, at the age of 16, he escaped and joined his mother in Stirling, where she was about to marry yet again (Henry VIII was not the only much-married Tudor).

The almost forgotten boy king turned out to be a man of character, with much charm, when he chose to exert it, but also with a less endearing streak of ruthlessness.

When he went to Paris in 1536 to marry the daughter of the Duke of Vendôme, he so disliked the look of his bride-to-be that he refused to go through with the ceremony! Tactfully, François I offered him one of his own daughters, Madeline. But the gentle Madeline survived only two months of the Scottish climate and James negotiated another French marriage to Mary of Guise, the formidable lady who became the mother of Mary, Queen of Scots.

James died at Falkland in 1542, just after he had heard of the birth of his daughter. He was 31 and had been king for 29 years. Once again Scotland had an infant sovereign.

MARY AND MARRIAGE

Henry VIII tried to arrange a marriage with his son, Edward, and when the Scots refused he responded with 'The Rough Wooing', a series of bloody and destructive raids on lowland Scotland, and, in 1548, the six-year-old Scottish Queen was sent to France. There 10 years later she married the Dauphin who was to become François II.

François died after only 17 months on the throne and, in 1561, Mary returned to Scotland, a tall red-haired girl of 18 who was instantly plunged into civil and religious strife. Her arguments with the reformer, John Knox, are famous and even he allowed her a modicum of grudging admiration.

But all her marriages were disastrous. Lord Darnley, related to the royal houses of both Scotland and England, was a dissolute fop, murdered in mysterious circumstances. The Earl of Bothwell was a self-seeking bully, and that marriage caused riots and civil war. Escaping from imprisonment in Loch Leven Castle, Mary lost her last battle at Langside near Glasgow and fled to England seeking asylum from her cousin, Queen Elizabeth.

There she found none of the solace nor support she sought.

Imprisoned for 19 years and finally executed at Fotheringay in 1587 on a charge of treason to a queen to whom she had never owed allegiance, her colourful and tragic story has held the world's imagination ever since.

Mary's son by Darnley, James VI of Scotland, became King of England when Elizabeth died in 1603. His departure for England, where he was known as James I, effectively marked the end of Edinburgh as a royal capital, although Scotland was to have its own Parliament for another hundred years.

James's second son came to Scotland to be crowned Charles I. During the Civil War the Marquis of Montrose fought a brilliant campaign to support the king, and after Charles's execution, the Lord Protector Cromwell came north to campaign against Charles II's attempt to regain the throne.

The last time the Scottish crown jewels, now in Edinburgh Castle, were used in a coronation ceremony was in 1651, when Charles II was crowned in Scone, a decade before his English coronation.

*Bonnie Prince Charlie,
encouraged by loyal
supporters, makes his way
up the narrow Royal Mile
to Edinburgh Castle*

LAST OF THE STUARTS

The last of the Stuart kings, James II of
England and VII of Scotland, came to
Edinburgh when he was Duke of York as
the King's Commissioner. It was not a
happy time in Scotland with the bloody
moorland battles being fought out
between the King's men and the
Covenanters, and James, the fanatical,
slightly deranged Catholic, was not the
man to solve these problems.

But oddly enough his only monument
in the city is a frivolous one. He played a
golf match on Leith Links with a local
shoemaker, John Paterstone, as his partner
against two English noblemen. The
winnings enabled Paterstone to build a
house called Golfer's Land in the
Canongate, and the plaque he placed on it,
inscribed with the sound golfing motto
'Far and Sure' can still be seen in the Royal
Mile today.

When James succeeded to the throne on
his brother's death in 1685, he immediately
began laying the foundations of his own
destruction by repealing all the laws
against Catholicism. In Edinburgh he
refurbished the Chapel Royal at Holyrood
for Catholic worship and installed a
printing press, operated by Jesuit priests,
in the palace at the foot of the Canongate.

When he fled to France after 'The
Glorious Revolution' of 1688, the
Edinburgh mob destroyed both.

From the Scottish Parliament, which
met in 1689 to decide whether or not to
accept William of Orange as king, grew
the idea of closer ties with England. In the
years of famine with which the 17th
century ended in Scotland, arguments in
favour of union with the prosperous
English were revived.

Protests and riots all over Scotland
greeted the proposals for the Union of the
Parliaments — Daniel Defoe, author of
Robinson Crusoe, who was spying for the
English Government in Edinburgh, left a
graphic account of these times — but the
Union went through in 1707 and the
Parliament of Scotland was no more.

PRINCE CHARLIE AND THE '45

Four Jacobite rebellions aimed at
restoring the exiled Stuarts to the throne
had their origins in Scotland and, in the
last of them in 1745, Bonnie Prince Charlie
and his Highlanders took Edinburgh and
crushed a Hanoverian army sent against
them under Sir John Cope at Prestonpans.

The Prince had his father proclaimed
king at the Mercat Cross in a document
which appointed himself as Prince Regent
and promised religious freedom to
Scotland and the abolition of the Act of
Union 'which has reduced Scotland to
being no more than an English province'.

After the Battle of Prestonpans, Prince
Charlie behaved with great humanity, in
stark contrast to the brutality of the Duke
of Cumberland after Culloden, and sent to
Edinburgh for surgeons to treat the
wounded of both sides.

One of the surgeons was John Rattray,
captain of the Company of Gentlemen
Golfers (now the Honourable Company
of Edinburgh Golfers, the oldest golf club
in the world), whose subsequent career
supremely illustrates the advantages of
belonging to a good club!

Taken prisoner at Culloden, he was
saved from the gallows by his fellow
member, Duncan Forbes, Lord President
of the Court of Session, the senior judge in
Scotland.

Two decades after Culloden, a new
spirit was abroad in Scotland. There was a
feeling of optimism, of renewed national
vigour and pride — at least in the
Lowlands.

There were developments in industry,
agriculture and trade and a flourishing of
literature, philosophy and the arts. James
Craig published his plan for the New Town
and Edinburgh became a centre of not
merely British but European significance.

A NEW AGE

In the latter half of the 18th century the Scottish Enlightenment marked an age when, suddenly, all human knowledge became accessible and there were men of genius everywhere to drink at its fountain.

The greatest of the Scottish philosophers, David Hume, was one of the first to live in the New Town, and a plaque in St Andrew Square marks the site of his house. The building of the New Town earned Edinburgh the description of 'the most exciting Georgian city in Britain'. An excellent example of early town-planning, it took the aristocrats and the top professional families of Edinburgh across the Nor'Loch to live in an elegant city of squares and crescents, beautifully proportioned classical buildings and green space. Nothing could have been a greater contrast to the packed, vibrant, semi-squalor of the Old Town.

Hume was only one of the protagonists of Edinburgh's 'Golden Age'. Painters like Ramsay, Nasmyth and Raeburn, poets such as Fergusson, the older Ramsay and Burns, novelists like Walter Scott, geologists like James Hutton, and architects such as Robert Adam and his brothers rubbed shoulders with the men who were revolutionising surgery, political economy, engineering, physics and a host of other subjects.

To Edinburgh came men of learning and distinction, drawn by its fame and its beauty — Dr Johnson, Jean Jacques Rousseau, Benjamin Franklin, Bismarck, Chopin, Mendelssohn and Hans Andersen among them.

The writings of Johnson and his ebullient biographer, James Boswell, and the enthusiasm of Queen Victoria and Prince Albert for scenery north of the Border made Scotland a desirable destination just at the time when the advent of rail travel made it a possible one.

The railway was one of the benefits which the Industrial Revolution brought to Edinburgh in the 19th century. It ran past the foot of the Castle Rock where the Nor'Loch had been drained.

EDINBURGH TODAY

At the beginning of the century the New Town was being completed. At its end some of the literary and philosophical glory had faded, but Edinburgh had become famous as a medical centre through Simpson's use of anaesthetics and Lister's work on antiseptics. Banking and insurance, printing and brewing were also part of Edinburgh's commercial spectrum.

The 20th century added electronics and light industry to the capital's portfolio, and with the creation of the Edinburgh Festival in 1947 a determined bid was made for cultural recognition again.

Edinburgh hosted the Commonwealth Games in 1970 and 1986, and the advent of the Festival has helped to make tourism a major industry. The increase in Edinburgh's status is reflected in its range of international contacts. The city is twinned with Dunedin, Florence, Munich, Nice, San Diego, Vancouver and the Chinese city of Xi'an.

Ultimately, however, Edinburgh's attraction is founded not on its associations but on itself. This is a city in which the vistas, the light and the ambience is constantly changing. Down its streets and through its vennels and wynds there are altering views from every corner — of the sea, the hills, a crenellation of towers and spires, a sweep of dramatic or elegant buildings.

Iain Crawford is a journalist and writer and has also been closely involved with the Edinburgh Festival.

NEW TOWN ELEGANCE
The building of Moray Place, with its distinctive Tuscan porticos, marked the third and final phase of the New Town. Built on what was the Earl of Moray's estate, the development was completed by 1827

SCOTT MONUMENT
A climb of 287 steps will take the hardy visitor to a spectacular viewpoint at the top

Capital Buildings

I n no other city in Britain can you see so dramatically contrasted the romantic glamour of a medieval burgh and the reasoned elegance of a Georgian town. In Edinburgh the two lie side by side, both now surrounded by a Victorian out-growth that is grand in itself.

An excellent starting point would be Greyfriars Churchyard, at the west end of the Kirk. Here, on the site of one of Edinburgh's pre-Reformation monasteries, is the city's architectural growth encapsulated. North is the Castle and the ridge-town of the medieval burgh; south is the line of the Old Town wall. To the west is the huge and magnificent presence of Heriot's Hospital, William Wallace's renaissance triumph, and east is the 1721 part of Greyfriars Church.

THE OLD TOWN

To really appreciate Edinburgh's architecture to the full, you have to walk. The Old Town is about a mile long, from Castle to Palace. Its oldest feature is its ground plan — the upper part best pictured as a fish's skeleton, a backbone of High Street and a fringe on either side of smaller bones — the wynds, closes and entries of our medieval town.

To get the feel of the character of these closes, walk into Riddle's Court (322–8 Lawnmarket) or venture a few yards down Old Fishmarket Close (188–90 High

Street). The courtyard buildings in Riddle's Court (1590) provide a good lesson in the Scottish vernacular style of building, common from the 16th to the 18th centuries for the homes of ordinary (but not poor) people. Buildings are of rubble stone, 'harled' (roughcast) on the outside for weather-proofing; layout of windows is unplanned, irregular and full of surprises.

Across the street from Riddle's Court is the high frontage of Gladstone's Land (c1620). The site is medieval in scope — the population's housing demands were intense, so that the only answer was to build high and narrow, piling house upon house in a vertical street. You can go into the lower floors (National Trust for Scotland) and appreciate the character of a painted interior of the 17th century.

John Knox's House (c1540) in the High Street and Huntly House (c1570) in the Canongate sum up the inconsistencies of the period — the varied building materials, from timber and plaster through stone-rubble to ashlar — and the delightful urge to gain upper floor space by throwing floors forward like protruding jetties.

MEDIEVAL TO BAROQUE

But what of grander styles? You can find Romanesque and Gothic in Edinburgh but you have to look for it. St Margaret's Chapel in the Castle is 12th-century Romanesque, and the ruined west façade of Holyrood is about a century later taking us forward into very early Gothic in a magnificently composed frontispiece. High Gothic of the 15th century is represented at its best (for Scotland) in the choir of St Giles, a finely grand arrangement of vaults and ribs and heraldry. But beyond these there are other treasures for the enthusiast: Duddingston Parish Church, a surviving village centre, has an excellent Norman structure and doorway, Corstorphine Church is a 15th-century collegiate foundation, and Restalrig Church (a map and a car are essential for this one) has a very fine hexagonal chapel of 1477 added by James III, ribbed and piered to make it a small masterpiece.

The best of architectural style in the Old Town is reserved for its public buildings. Visit Heriot's Hospital quadrangle (1628), off Lauriston Place, and admire the sculptural decoration (scenes of childhood and philanthropy) over the north portal. Enter (except on Mondays) the law-courts off Parliament Square to enjoy Scotland's grandest 17th-century interior — the Parliament Hall of 1632, a vast gathering place under a magnificent hammer-beam roof of Danish oak. Step across the High Street from here to look, at least from the outside, at the City Chambers of 1753, a dourly classical façade by John Adam.

By far the most important secular building in the Old Town is the Palace of Holyroodhouse, built in the 1670s by Sir William Bruce for King Charles II — who never came. Bruce's quadrangle, its ranges of rooms set above open arcades, is a model in correct use of the classical orders. Corinthian rises from Ionic upon a Doric lower floor and the whole is topped by a 'Scottish' frieze and a royally embellished pediment. Before Robert Adam and William Adam, his father, whose work scarcely survives in Edinburgh, Bruce, who died in 1710, was Scotland's best known architect.

Bruce's interiors at Holyrood form a *Grand Appartement* which represents baroque at its richest interpretation in Scotland. The rooms are arranged (typically for the period) in *enfilade*, and in the King's Bedroom they reach a pitch of perfection unrivalled in Scotland. The plasterwork, deep and satisfying, the wood-carving (Gibbons-like), and the inserted decorative painting are all by Dutch craftsmen invited across by Bruce.

THE CLASSICAL NEW TOWN

Edinburgh is proud of its New Towns. Taken together these Georgian developments from 1767 to about 1840 form the largest urban conservation area in Britain, and at the Conservation Centre, 13A Dundas Street, you will find excellent literature and displays on the New Towns. The elegant streets and squares and private gardens are to be enjoyed first for their proportions and their rational symmetry, secondly for the classical perfection of their individual buildings.

The town planners who created all this were various. There was the relatively unknown James Craig, who pioneered it all in 1767 with a rigorously unadventurous gridiron that turns upon the St Andrews Square — George Street — Charlotte Square spine. Then came Robert Reid and William Sibbald, who added the second New Town in parallel and to the north, with spinal Great King Street linking Drummond Place with Royal Circus. From the 1820s, the third New Town, to the west, was conceived by James Gillespie Graham with the grandest of polygons, circles and semi-circles. Moray Place represents the peak of New Town grandiloquence.

PARLIAMENT SQUARE

Seen here from Parliament House with St Giles Cathedral behind, this statue of Charles II, dated 1685, is one of the oldest equestrian statues in Britain.

Other town planners contributed beyond this triple core: W H Playfair in the Calton Hill terraces, and James Milne in the Stockbridge streets, formerly on Sir Henry Raeburn's estate. It may be impossible to explore all these but, for a quiet discreet cameo of off-centre Georgian style, walk up James Milne's Saxe-Coburg Street (1821) past his elegant little St Bernard's Church and round the Place at the top-end.

What of the individual buildings? There is an overriding New Town house style, uniformly fronted, with basement, three storeys and attic. Front doors are beautifully fanlighted, windows are precisely positioned and astragalled in panes four up and three across (though Victorian and later taste have often changed these). The street-level façade is 'rusticated' with channelled ashlar, and elegant railings, sometimes with restored light brackets, guard the basements.

With the possible exception of 8 Queen Street by Robert Adam, you need not worry about individual architects; these houses were just the normal expectation of an urban gentleman and any one of a dozen skilled builders could do the job — at a price. The north side of Charlotte Square (1791), of course, is something different, for here — for the first time — a notable architect, Robert Adam, imposed his own wishes and his highly elaborate elevation upon whoever came to build on this street-terrace site. As a result this 11-house block is one of the triumphs of 18th-century informed taste. It has compositional majesty, — Nos 5, 6 and 7 are emphasised as centrepieces, and Nos 1–2 and 10–11 are blocked forward, garlanded and sphynxed just as you would expect Robert Adam to do.

ROBERT ADAM AND AFTER

Robert Adam was not much involved in domestic house building in Edinburgh, unlike his rival William Chambers who built Dundas House (1771 — now the Royal Bank) in St Andrew Square, well worth two glances, and Duddingston House in the suburbs, sadly, scarcely worth one. His Edinburgh *métier* lay in his public buildings; notably, the circular monument to David Hume in the Calton Burial Ground, the massive Register House at Princes Street's east end, and the University on South Bridge. Register House (1774) is monumental, its plan as a repository for Scotland's records owing not a little to Robert Adam's memory of vast Roman baths. It is worth braving the security men (if the notice declares only 'Black Alert') and going in to enjoy the superb interior of the Dome, carefully rehabilitated some years ago to Adam's colour values.

The University's Old College was started by Robert Adam in 1789, and finished by W H Playfair about 1830. Playfair was the dominant figure in late Georgian and Victorian Edinburgh, and it is worth going in to the University's Art Centre, or to its Library Hall (south side) to see how Adam's restrained classicism grows in magisterial character with Playfair under the influence of Victorian self-aggrandisement.

Playfair was Scotland's leading neo-Greek. On Princes Street his Royal Scottish Academy (built 1822–36) is a most enjoyable Greek Doric style. But for Playfair's Athens Revisited go up to the top of the Calton Hill and enjoy his classical collection. His ravishing version of the Lysicrates monument (1831) commemorates Professor Dugald Stewart, his Greek Doric block commemorates his uncle, Professor John Playfair, and his unfinished National Monument (1826), which was to have replicated the Parthenon, would have commemorated practically everybody else.

VICTORIAN EDINBURGH

It is when you go out into the inner suburbs that Victorian taste runs riot. Edinburgh has always been a great place for schools and hospital-schools and — following the model of 17th-century Heriot's Hospital — a great anthology of these was achieved in the 19th century, each wilder than the next. You need a car to search these out but for sheer architectural extravaganza it is worth the effort. Playfair built the largest of them all — Donaldson's Hospital (1841) on the main road west from Haymarket. It is a sort of Hardwick Hall and Burghley House rolled into one and might easily be mistaken by a *revenant* King Charles I for a Royal Palace; in fact it is a school for the deaf. The Orphan Hospital (1831, now Dean Education Centre) on Belford Road is neo-baroque by Thomas Hamilton, and it faces the neo-Greek Watson's Hospital (1825, now the Gallery of Modern Art) by William Burn. Hamilton and Burn were notable contemporaries and, at least in part, expert neo-classicists; Burn otherwise excelled in country houses. Finally, there are Daniel Stewart's Hospital (1848 by David Rhind) on Queensferry Road and Fettes College (1864 by David Bryce), visible half a mile to the north, which together — Scottish Jacobean facing French chateauvian — are probably the least functional school buildings ever built, but, nevertheless, grand eye-stoppers across the suburban townscape.

Edinburgh has nothing to match the *fin-de-siècle* advance into modern times pioneered in Glasgow by Charles Rennie Mackintosh, but his contemporary Sir Robert Lorimer (died 1929), who excelled in reviving the vanishing craftsmanship of architectural decoration, is represented by two outstanding buildings. One is the Thistle Chapel, the south-east appendage to St Giles added in 1910 and a triumph of High Gothic revival. The wood carving, metal work and tincturing show the achievement of Lorimer in creating an 'Edinburgh School of Craftsmanship', a salutary rival to the reputation of the 'Glasgow Boys'. Lorimer's other great building is on Edinburgh Castle, the immensely reverential, immensely moving national shrine to the memory of Scotland's recent fallen. In its steely, unbending restraint, classical in its dignity, it must surpass any other commemorative architect's creation.

MODERN TIMES

So finally to today! What can we encourage the visitor to enjoy among post-war additions to the Edinburgh scene? There are some you should not see (if you can help it): for ill-sited brutalism, the Grassmarket's Mountbatten Building, Holyrood Road's Moray House Gymnasium, and Leith Street's St James's Centre take a lot of beating. In contrast, the newest Festival Square, facing the Usher Hall on Lothian Road will be glossy and painlessly acceptable when it is finally squared off. The Scottish Widows Fund building (1972) on Dalkeith Road is very exciting in its polygonal design, echoing the nearby basaltic polygons of Arthur's Seat. Indeed the Commonwealth Pool next door (1967) has a clean-cut presentation much to be admired. But praise in modern building activity in Edinburgh must also be given to the often small-scale in-fills that take place on Old Town sites. Off the Canongate or the High Street — as at Chessel's Court or, very recently, the Museum of Childhood building — new structures have appeared that are entirely sensitive to pre-conditions of scale and the vernacular tradition.

On the whole, Edinburgh's architectural inheritance is in good hands. The New Town Committee, the Old Town Committee, both armed with statutory teeth, and the powerful over all watchdog, the Cockburn Association, present an informed strength of opinion that it will take more than an ordinary developer to overcome.

But a heritage needs appreciation, and it is the awareness of value and the appreciation of merit by the visitor that will help Edinburgh to remain an architectural treasury of great worth.

Basil Skinner is Director of Extra-mural Studies at Edinburgh University.

NEW FOR OLD
What was once a rather shabby exhibition hall above the Waverley Station has been transformed into a smart high-class shopping mall

The Royal Mile

T he hard, spiky spine of the Old Town, the Royal Mile is one of the most famous and historic thoroughfares in the world where riots have spilled across the streets, clansmen battled and nobles duelled and rich and poor, obscure and famous, shared the cramped but lively democracy of life in tall tenements.

Much more than the lofty vistas of the New Town the Royal Mile retains the flavour of Scotland's ancient capital, once a settlement of gaunt tenements — Europe's first skyscrapers — some as high as 16 storeys. In the mid-18th century, about 50,000 people were crammed in the Royal Mile's tenements and in adjoining narrow streets, the rich on the upper floors for the best air, the poor on the lower ones.

Here, poets Robert Burns and Robert Fergusson drank with the literati in taverns and clubs, the poet, bookseller and wigmaker, Allan Ramsay, kept his shop and, among other lofty intellects, David Hume, philosopher and historian, and Adam Smith, author of *The Wealth of Nations*, lived.

1 Walkers, starting downwards, at Castlehill on the Esplanade are, because of a legal fiction by King Charles I, (1625–49), standing on what was Nova Scotia soil. So as to create the orders of Knight-baronet of Scotland and Nova Scotia and because of the difficulties of carrying out the investiture ceremony in Nova Scotia, the King made the Esplanade part of the colony for that purpose. At the Esplanade entrance a plaque commemorates witch-burnings; more took place there than anywhere else in Scotland.

2 The first significant building is Cannon Ball house (*right*), once a merchant's house, dated 1630 and so named because the ball lodged in the west wall may have been fired from the castle at the Jacobite siege of 1745. More probably it marks the gravitation height of Edinburgh's first piped water supply to the area in 1681.

3 A diversion (*left*) down Ramsay Lane to Ramsay Gardens, shows fantastic, turreted houses. The area was named after the poet, Allan Ramsay, who, about 1740, built an octagonal house, known to local wits as the 'Goose Pie'. His son, also named Allan, a portrait painter to King George III, erected more houses. At the end of the

last century, Sir Patrick Geddes, the pioneering town-planner who did much to rehabilitate the Royal Mile, remodelled buildings romantically to lure back university teachers and students to the Old Town.

4 Again at Castlehill is Boswell's Court, (*right*) named after Dr John Boswell, medical practitioner and uncle of James Boswell, Dr Johnson's biographer. The great lexicographer is said to have dined there with the two Boswells.

5 On the left is the castellated Outlook Tower with its Camera Obscura offering fascinating views of Edinburgh. The building's lower part is 17th century; the upper parts were added in 1853 when it was known as Short's Observatory. Near the end of the last century, Sir Patrick Geddes developed the building as a sociological museum when it was given its present name.

6 Further down (*right*) is the Gothic Tolbooth St John's Church. Completed in 1844, it served, until recently, the city's Highland community. Its 241ft spire is the highest in Edinburgh.

7 At the Lawnmarket, once a bustling cross between a country fair and an Indian camp is Upper Bow (*right*), the head of one of the Old Town's most characteristic winding streets, now mainly demolished. Here was the house of Major Thomas Weir, commander of the City Guard, a pious church member who, with his sister, Grizel, confessed to dealing in witchcraft. Both were strangled and burned in 1670, the Major's ghost on a headless black horse being reported in the area for years afterwards.

8 Opposite, Mylne's Court and James' Court were attempts to bring fresh air into the area by demolishing old tenements and rebuilding others to form open squares. The first, built in 1690 by Robert Mylne, Master Mason to the King, is now a

Gladstone's Land

cheat death by wearing an iron collar under his shirt but failed.

13 At the intersection of George IV Bridge and Bank Street and into High Street are (*on the right*) three brass plates marking the city's last public hanging in 1864. William Burke, who with Hare sold to anatomists the bodies of people they murdered, was hanged there in 1828.

14 On the right is Parliament Square with Parliament House, built in 1639, where the Scottish parliament and courts met until the union of the Scottish and English parliaments in 1707, and which now houses the High Court, Court of Session and Signet Library. The square, with the only representation of Charles II on horseback, was once 'the busiest and most populous nook of the old town'.

15 A heart-shaped pattern of setts in the west square marks the site of the Old Tolbooth. Demolished in 1817, it served for over 400 years as council chamber, courthouse, place of execution and tolls' collection. It is an Edinburgh custom to spit on the spot.

16 St Giles, the High Kirk of Edinburgh, with its superb crown tower, is the most dominant building in the Old Town. John Knox, the fiery verbal scourge of Mary, Queen of Scots, was appointed minister after the Reformation, and it was the scene of riot in 1637 when reforms, introduced by Charles I were claimed to savour of popery. Jenny Geddes, a vegetable seller, is said to have hurtled a stool at the Bishop of Edinburgh who dared 'sing masse in my lugge' (ear).

17 On the opposite side is Advocates Close, one of the most picturesque of Edinburgh's alleyways and once so narrow that residents could almost shake hands with those opposite. Sir James Stewart, the Lord Advocate, lived there from 1692 to 1713.

18 A few yards down from St Giles, the Mercat Cross contains in its shaft part of the original 15th-century cross — its site marked nearby on the roadway — at which many famous Scots were executed. The present cross, erected in 1885, is still the scene of royal proclamations.

19 The neo-classical City Chambers opposite was completed in 1761 as the Royal Exchange. In 1811 it was used by the municipal authorities and later expanded; its 12-storey rear in Cockburn Street is one of the tallest surviving Old Town buildings.

university hall of residence. The second, built in 1725 by James Brownhill, was described by the philosopher, David Hume, as 'very elegant but too small to display my great talent for cookery'.

9 A short way down the same side, Gladstone's Land, an older property acquired in 1617 by Thomas Gledstanes, an Edinburgh merchant and burgess, is the best-preserved example of a 17th-century house in the Old Town. Owned and renovated by the National Trust for Scotland, it is furnished in authentic 17th-century style.

10 Lady Stair's House (1622) (*left*) became, early in the 18th century, the house of Eleanor, Countess of Stair. A hole under the fore-stair of the house once provided shelter for the family sow. The house is now a Robert Burns, Sir Walter Scott and Robert Louis Stevenson museum. In 1786 Burns lived in a house in the close.

11 Across the street is 16th-century Riddle's Court. Here Bailie MacMorran lived, one of the richest men in his time. He was shot dead in 1595 by High School boys as he tried to restore order during a pupils' riot over reduced holidays.

12 Further down is Brodie's Close, home of William Brodie, town councillor and Deacon of the Wrights, upright citizen by day but burglar by night to pay off gambling debts and support two mistresses and five illegitimate children.

He was hanged on October 1, 1788 by a gibbet to which he had earlier made improvements. Brodie, the inspiration for Stevenson's *Dr Jekyll and Mr Hyde*, tried to

A wall plaque past the courtyard shows what was the entrance to Craig's Close, the site of the Cape Club, numbering some of Edinburgh's most famous citizens among its membership, including the poet, Robert Fergusson. On the same side is Anchor Close, the meeting place of the Crochallan Fencibles, a club for 'men of original character and talent.' Burns was introduced to it in 1787 by his printer, William Smellie, whose premises were in the close and who printed the *Encyclopaedia Britannica's* first edition in 1768.

20 Across the street is the Old Assembly Close where fashionable balls were held in the Old Assembly Rooms; Oliver Goldsmith remarked on the gaiety of them and the beauty of the girls there. A few yards down is New Assembly Close, where dancing assemblies were also held; it is now the site of the Waxworks Museum.

21 The elegant Countess of Eglinton — to whom Allan Ramsay dedicated his pastoral drama, *The Gentle Shepherd* — and her seven beautiful daughters, whose procession of sedan chairs to dancing assemblies always drew crowds, lived opposite at Old Stamp Close. Here Flora Macdonald, who saved Prince Charlie from the pursuing government troops, went to school.

22 On the right is the Tron Kirk, named after a nearby public weigh beam or *tron*. Completed around 1648, its original wooden steeple stood until 1824 when its destruction by fire was like a 'beautiful firework'. The fine hammer-beam roof survived and a new stone spire was built in 1828. Here, Edinburgh traditionally celebrates the New Year. The church was closed in 1952.

23 Crossing the North Bridge and South Bridge intersection on the left is Carrubber's Close, once a Jacobites' haunt. John Spottiswood, Archbishop of St Andrews and Scots historian (1565–1639), who crowned Charles I at Holyrood in 1633, lived here. Allan Ramsay had a shop and opened a theatre here in 1736 but closed it after puritanical magistrates refused a licence.

24 Further down are Bailie Fyfe's Close and Paisley Close. In 1861, a tenement between them collapsed, killing 35 occupants. Rescuers found a trapped boy who shouted, 'Heave awa' chaps. I'm no deid yet'. The incident is commemorated by a sculpture of the boy's face and an inscription.

25 On the other side is the Museum of Childhood, an imaginative collection of old and new toys.

26 Moubray House (*left*) where Daniel Defoe, author of *Robinson Crusoe* and suspected English spy, lived and edited the *Edinburgh Courant* in 1710. One of the oldest city houses, dated perhaps 1462, with characteristic outside stair, it was once a tavern; now it is a private house.

27 Nearby is John Knox's House, one of the oldest (about 1490) and most distinctive buildings in the Old Town. The preacher is believed to have occupied it between 1561 and 1572, though perhaps only for three months. In 1571 a musket was fired through a window, the ball lodging in the ceiling of the room in which he sat. The house was earlier owned in 1556 by James Mossman, goldsmith to Mary, Queen of Scots, and his wife, Mariota Arres.

28 Opposite is Hyndford's Close, where Jean Maxwell lived, wife of Alexander, Duke of Gordon (1743–1827). A beauty and leader of fashion, Scott said her 'sole claim to wit rested upon her brazen impudence and disregard to the feelings of all who were near her'.

29 On the same side is Tweeddale Court, once the mansion of Dame Margaret Kerr, wife of the 7th Lord Hay of Yester. It became the British Linen Bank's head office, and, in a famous murder, a bank porter, William Begbie, was stabbed to death there in 1806 by an unknown person and robbed of £4,392. In 1817, the bank was succeeded by Oliver & Boyd publishers, who occupied it until 1973. The Scottish Poetry Library is here.

30 Lower right is World's End Close, the last close before the old city wall and the outside world — in this case the Canongate, meaning the way of the monks walking to Edinburgh from Holyrood Abbey. Once highly fashionable, in 1769 it could still boast among its residents: 2 dukes, 16 earls, 7 barons, 7 judges and 13 baronets. When the royal family went to London after the union of the Scottish and English crowns in 1603, many of the nobility followed and the area slowly declined. A few of their houses remain.

31 Moray House, (*right*) built in 1628, now a teacher training college, was owned by the Earls of Moray and famed for its elegant gardens. Charles I visited it and Cromwell made it his headquarters in 1648. The Treaty of Union was signed here by the 'parcel of rogues.'

32 Downwards, on the same side is Huntly House, a fine 1570 dwelling, once the home of the Dowager Countess of Gordon, and now the city museum.

33 Bakehouse Close, nearby, is a favourite of artists, and richly evokes the atmosphere of the Old Town.

34 Adjoining, Acheson House is a superb example of a 17th-century baronial town house and now the Scottish Craft Centre.

35 On the left is the 1591 Scoto-French-style Canongate Tolbooth. Formerly a council chamber, courthouse, jail and collection place for burgh dues, it is now a museum.

36 Further down is the Canongate Church, built in 1688. English soldiers taken prisoner by Prince Charlie's army after his victory at Prestonpans were held there. Those buried in the churchyard include the poet, Robert Fergusson, Mrs Agnes McLehose, Burns's 'Clarinda' and Professor James Gregory, compounder of the purgative, Gregory's Mixture.

37 Still descending, one sees Whitefoord House (*left*), which takes its name from Sir John Whitefoord (died 1803), now a veterans' residence.

38 Opposite is Queensberry House, where the second Duke of Queensberry accepted a bribe of £12,325 to push through the Treaty of Union. His eldest son 'an insane monster', roasted a kitchen boy alive on a spit and was eating him when he was discovered. It is now an old people's hospital.

39 Left is White Horse Close, a 1964 restoration of 17th-century houses and coaching inn, the last said to be the quarters for Prince Charlie's officers during his 1745 occupation of the city.

40 Then comes Abbey Strand and the walk ends at the gates leading to Holyrood Palace.

The distance from the drawbridge at Edinburgh Castle to the door of Holyrood Palace is 1 mile 106yd.

Albert Morris is a journalist and writes a regular column for The Scotsman.

HUNTLY HOUSE
A copy of the National Covenant, signed in Greyfriars Churchyard in 1638, is among the many items of historic interest in this small city museum

wynd: ways that are open from both ends
close: an entry back or front, to a tenement
land: tenement block of flats
court: a courtyard surrounded by buildings and **pens:** archway

Edinburgh's Villages

A s cities expand, they tend to engulf existing communities. Dozens of villages have been swamped in the Scottish capital's development from an overcrowded community in the protective shelter of the Castle to the modern metropolis of Greater Edinburgh, which now covers an area of 51 square miles. In many cases, only traces of the original villages remain: in others, they survive as places with a character and an identity of their own.

James Gillespie

CRAMOND

The picturesque village of Cramond, at the mouth of the River Almond, is one of the most popular spots for visitors, with its trim old white houses and quaint little courtyards off an alley running at right angles to the river. Equally trim and welcoming is the nearby hostelry, Cramond Inn, which dates from 1670.

There are few obvious signs that Cramond in the 18th century was the hub of a busy industrial area, not only milling grain — which it had done from at least 1178 — but processing cloth, producing paper and pioneering in iron manufacture.

Very much earlier — about AD142 — the Romans established a fort at Cramond, part of which has been excavated to the north of Cramond Kirk. A plan of the fort can be found adjacent to the church, which has medieval origins. The oldest part of the present church is its 15th-century tower.

Cramond Tower, a medieval stronghold, has been comprehensively restored. Between the tower and the churchyard is another historic building, Cramond House, which dates from 1680. Once the home of the Inglis family, lairds for generations, it is now owned by Cramond Kirk and used in part by the National Trust for Scotland.

Following the Almond inland from its estuary is the River Almond Walkway which lead to the remains of Fair-a-Far Mill and its weir (see pp 62–3).

A small ferryboat makes the short crossing of the River Almond to provide a pleasant walk in the grounds of Lord Rosebery's estate of Dalmeny to Queensferry.

In the summer, exhibitions are mounted by the Cramond Heritage Trust in the Old Maltings.

CRAMOND
Just a few miles from the hustle and bustle of city life, it is small wonder that this peaceful haven is such a popular spot with Edinburgh folk, particularly the boating fraternity!

COLINTON

Colinton, on the southern outskirts of the city, is today one of the most prosperous suburbs. It became a busy little place when the waters that tumbled through the beautiful wooded Colinton Dell were harnessed to turn the wheels of grain, flax, paper and snuff mills.

At the heart of village life was Colinton Parish Church. The present church, which dates from 1771 (though substantially altered since), is the successor to the Kirk of the Hailes, mentioned as early as 1097.

Charity was a strong tradition in Colinton. One notable benefactor was James Gillespie of Spylaw, who owned a nearby snuff mill and made a fortune from it. He founded a hospital bearing his name, also a free school for the education of poor boys. Gillespie's mausoleum is in the churchyard.

The church, its manse and garden, have strong associations with Robert Louis Stevenson. His maternal grandfather, the Rev Dr Lewis Balfour, was the parish minister from 1823 to 1860 and Stevenson spent many happy boyhood days at the manse, exercising his vivid imagination in the garden and around the mills.

The 19th century brought big changes to Colinton — a decline of the mills as steam power ousted water power, but an influx of new residents as a branch line of the Caledonian Railway brought the village within commuting range of Edinburgh. Many handsome villas were built, their architects including Sir Robert Lorimer.

Among historic buildings in the Colinton area are Colinton Castle (built 1450), now a ruin in the grounds of Merchiston Castle School, and the Covenanters' Monument in Redford Road.

DEAN VILLAGE

In complete contrast to the formal layout and classical order of the New Town is Dean Village, only five minutes or so from the west end of Princes Street. Before Thomas Telford's mighty Dean Bridge opened an easier road to Queensferry and the north, the route lay through one of the oldest villages in the city with milling associations dating back to the 12th century. Now known as Dean Village, it is entered by the steep Bell's Brae.

For centuries it was the domain of millers and bakers. The Incorporation of Baxters (bakers), a powerful Edinburgh guild, at one time operated 11 watermills and two granaries in the area. They have left their marks for the observant to spot. At the head of Bell's Brae is Kirkbrae House, on one side of which is a sculptured panel bearing symbols of the bakers' art, wheatsheafs and a ripening sun; also the inscription, from Genesis: 'In the sweat of thy face shalt thou eat bread', and the date 1619. It is believed to have come from a group of old mill buildings called Jerico, which stood in nearby Miller Row. Three millstones supporting each other are a memorial to its past.

At the foot of Bell's Brae is a 17th-century building, a former meeting place of the baxters, with more craft symbols including crossed peels (shovels for extracting hot bread from the oven) and the crumbling inscription: 'God bless the Baxters of Edinburgh who built this House 1675'.

The Incorporation of Weavers was also active in the village in the early 18th century. As milling and weaving declined, a number of tanneries came into prominence. Other local industries included distilling and brewing.

Today, much of Dean Village is residential and if it lacks the bustle of industry and even the shops which add life to an area, its situation in picturesque surroundings so near the heart of the city makes it a popular place to live.

Hawthorn Buildings, half-timbered on the upper floor and with walls of yellow ochre, is one example of imaginative 19th-century housing. Another is Well Court, built in 1884 by John R Findlay,

proprietor of The *Scotsman*.

Much of Dean Village's charm is due to the rugged topography, the green banks of the Water of Leith, and the soaring arches of Telford's bridge. The graceful tower of the former Holy Trinity (Episcopal) Church, at the north end of the Dean Bridge, is another feature of a striking skyline.

STOCKBRIDGE

If the disappearance of Dean Village's shops robbed it of a true village atmosphere, that is not the case with its downstream neighbour, Stockbridge, a rural hamlet until the 18th century.

Stockbridge has been the spawning ground of writers, historians and artists, the most famous of whom was the portrait painter, Sir Henry Raeburn, born in 1756. A poor boy, orphaned at the age of six, he won fame and fortune from his painting, returning to the area to occupy St Bernard's, the principal mansion in old Stockbridge. From about 1813 he developed his own estate with property centred around the elegant Ann Street, named after his wife.

David Roberts, another prominent Stockbridge painter born in 1796, became, like Raeburn, a Royal Academician. He lived at 17th-century Duncan's Land in Church Street, now a restaurant of character.

Notable buildings around Stockbridge include Playfair's St Stephen's Church and, in Henderson Row, the original Edinburgh Academy building opened in 1824. Adjacent is a former school for deaf children. This was taken over in 1977 by Edinburgh Academy but some years earlier featured as the fictional 'Marcia Blane School for Girls' in the 20th Century Fox classic film of Edinburgh attitudes and school life, *The Prime of Miss Jean Brodie*.

One of Stockbridge's more interesting housing developments is known as 'The Colonies', constructed around 1861 by an Edinburgh building co-operative to provide low-cost housing for artisans.

CITY CENTRE VILLAGE

Many of the humble weavers' cottages and shops have been replaced by sympathetically designed flats and villas, and other buildings have been restored for residential or office use. The 12th-century Dean Village is thriving once more. The Water of Leith Walkway goes through the village and there are plans to extend it to the outskirts of the city

LEITH

A far cry from industrial days gone by, the docksides of Leith's inner port are now the scene of an altogether more leisurely trade—trendy waterfront restaurants and pubs

LEITH

Though Leith — which for centuries was Scotland's chief port — has been part of Greater Edinburgh since 1920 and from medieval times has rarely been free of the capital's control, it is the only district of the city where the inhabitants talk about 'going to Edinburgh' when they make the 1½-mile journey to the city centre. It has always had a strong sense of local identity.

The original port of Leith grew up around the Shore, where the Water of Leith joins the River Forth. Early trade included the export of salt fish and hides and the import of wine from Bordeaux. A flourishing ship-building industry grew up. The *Sirius*, launched in 1837, was the first steamship to cross the Atlantic.

The industrial revolution brought new industries to Leith, including sugar-refining and glass-making. To cope with increased trade and bigger vessels, a succession of new docks was built — Victoria (1851), Albert (1869), Edinburgh (1881) and Imperial (1903).

The population expanded rapidly but the depression which followed World War I and industrial decline after World War II made Leith an unemployment black spot. A lot of post-war housing was unimaginative to say the least. Nevertheless, much of interest remains in Leith and there are signs of a distinct upturn in its fortunes. The 200-year-old commercial area of Constitution Street and Bernard Street is unique and has been spruced up. Sympathetic restoration of historic buildings in the area includes Andrew Lamb's House in Burgess Street, a fine example of a prosperous merchant's house of the early 17th century. Also the early 18th-century King's Wark, taking its name from a much older one on the site, established in the 15th century by James I of Scotland for handling ordnance and cargoes for Royal use.

Also in the historic Shore area is an attractive modern housing development called King's Landing which successfully echoes features of older Scottish domestic architecture. 'King's Landing' commemorates the fact that George IV made a ceremonious landing at the old port when he visited Edinburgh in 1822 (quite an event since he was the first British monarch to visit Scotland for over 100 years). Leith had had many earlier Royal visitors including the young Mary Queen of Scots when she landed there to take the Scottish throne.

Leith Links, round which are some of Leith's better houses, has notable connections with archery and golf. Though there is no golf course there now, it was a popular game at the Links for centuries.

NEWHAVEN

The fishing village of Newhaven, just a mile west of Leith, enjoyed a brief period of glory in the 16th century when James IV, at war with England, had ambitions to build up a strong Scottish navy. Because of its deep water, Newhaven was chosen as the site of a new shipyard where a number of vessels were built, the most remarkable being the *Great Michael*, launched in 1511 as the Scottish flagship.

Newhaven reverted to its role of fishing village after the Battle of Flodden, where James IV was killed and Scotland's naval ambitions were abandoned. Apart from fish, there were massive oyster beds in the Firth of Forth and Newhaven enjoyed a monopoly in supplying oysters to the city of Edinburgh. These were immensely popular in the 18th and early 19th centuries but over-fishing eventually destroyed the beds. Herring were often abundant and, until quite recent times, Newhaven 'fishwives' were commonly seen in Edinburgh streets in traditional costume and carrying on their backs creels of fish which they sold on the streets or door-to-door. Newhaven's fishing activities declined in the 1950s and the last of its fishwives to trade traditionally disappeared about 1977.

The flavour of old Newhaven remains, for fisherfolk's cottages have either been restored or replaced by cottages which retain traditional features.

The Peacock Hotel is a hostelry established by an 18th-century wine merchant.

DUDDINGSTON

Close to the bird sanctuary of Duddingston Loch in Holyrood Park is Duddingston village, part of the new, quite extensive, suburban district of Duddingston. The 12th-century Duddingston Kirk stands near the park entrance.

Parallel with busy Old Church Lane, in a street called The Causeway, stands a former tavern where Bonnie Prince Charlie resided before his victory at the Battle of Prestonpans in 1745. From a state of dereliction this building has been restored as a private house by Duddingston Preservation Society. The Causeway is relatively quiet and secluded and Duddingston today exudes an orderly prosperity it did not know in the past. Apart from farm work, coal-heaving and flax-weaving were the mainstays of the village.

Duddingston has an ancient pub, the Sheep's Heid Inn, with origins in the 14th century, though the present building is only about 200 years old. The inn has the oldest skittle alley in Scotland, used for decades by the Trotters' Club, founded by Edinburgh journalists.

The 'roarin game' of curling has been played in Edinburgh for a very long time but its most popular venue in the late 18th and much of the 19th centuries was Duddingston Loch, following the formation of Duddingston Curling Society in 1795.

CORSTORPHINE

The old village of Corstorphine, in what is now one of the largest districts of the city, grew up around 14th-century Corstorphine Castle, stronghold of the Forrester family. Nothing remains of the castle, but its beehive-shaped dovecote with nests for over 1,000 birds (winter food for the laird) is intact.

Corstorphine Kirk with its distinctive stone-slabbed roof has an unusual square tower dating from the early 15th century. Church-goers were directed to worship not only by a bell but by a beacon light on the east gable, in regular use from 1429 until 1769. An electric light now occupies the niche.

Really old buildings in Corstorphine are few, but one that has survived from the mid-17th century is the Dower House in St Margaret's Park, a three-storey building with crowstepped gables built by the Forrester family.

A very old sycamore tree near the dovecote was the scene of a violent quarrel one night in 1679 between a former Lord Forrester and his paramour, Christian Nimmo, who drew the sword from her lover's scabbard and ran him through. For his murder she was executed in Edinburgh two months later. The tree still stands, the subject of inevitable ghost stories.

In the mid-18th century Corstorphine was famous for its Physic Well, at the east end of the village. The site is marked by a number of flat stones in a wood near Dunsmuir Court.

SWANSTON

Few thatched cottages survive in Scotland but an attractive group that constituted the original village of Swanston, in the foothills of the Pentland Hills, was restored in the late 1950s.

By a gate from the village on to the hills is a seat commemorating the distinguished poet, Edwin Muir (1887–1959), who loved the spot. So, as a young man, did Robert Louis Stevenson, whose summer home from 1867 to 1880 was the handsome bow-windowed Swanston Cottage, about a quarter of a mile away. Notebook and pencil in hand, the teenage RLS questioned and cultivated the villagers, making a special friend of John Tod, the 'roaring' shepherd.

Swanston Cottage and its environs feature in *St Ives*, in *Picturesque Notes* and the poem *Ille Terrarum*. The Pentlands, his *Hills of Home*, he remembered with nostalgia and wrote about from far-off Samoa, where he died.

The newer part of Swanston dates from around 1900 when farming was labour-intensive. Between the visitors' car park and the village is the historic farmhouse. In the 17th century it was a house of refuge for the Covenanters who fought the efforts of the Stuart monarchs to establish an Episcopalian form of church government in Scotland. Substantially rebuilt in the 18th century, Swanston farmhouse has now been converted into flats and has some modern additions.

Jim Bowman was the motoring correspondent of The Scotsman *until his recent retirement.*

DUDDINGSTON LOCH
Swans have nested here since 1680. Other birds to be seen at this attractive bird sanctuary include Brent geese, pochard, mallard and teal

SWANSTON
*'Here aft hae I, wi sober heart
For meditation sat apart.'
R L Stevenson on Swanston*

The Festival
&
the Arts

When the Edinburgh Festival began in 1947 it was a gesture of cultural defiance in a world made weary by war, misery and destruction.

Britain was still in a period of belt-tightening austerity, food was rationed and one of my most vivid memories of the first Festival is conducting famished and bemused opera singers from countries which were supposed to have lost the war, to Edinburgh's best black market restaurants.

Quite a number of the sedate citizens of Edinburgh — and elsewhere — thought that the City Fathers of Scotland's capital were quite mad to have got themselves involved in the expense and complexity of producing the world's leading international arts festival in such parlous times.

But from the first there was nothing small-minded or penny-pinching about the Festival idea. If there was to be a Festival in the magnificent setting of Edinburgh, then it had to be planned and run on a scale worthy of the city itself.

The world of the arts in the largest sense was the source of Edinburgh programmes and has remained so. Nothing which impinges on the imaginative and creative element in man has been ignored.

ALL THE ARTS
Edinburgh is an across-the-board Festival, happily and generously embracing all the arts.

It is almost impossible to name a great contemporary orchestra, artist, theatre or dance company which has not appeared in Edinburgh at Festival time. August in Edinburgh is the time when you wonder what the rest of the world is doing — because everyone who matters seems to be here.

Mark you, the canny burghers of Scotland's capital did not arrive at this state of cultural euphoria in one easy leap. They were as dazed as anyone at what happened in the city in that splendid summer of 1947.

The first Festival took place in brilliant sunshine and Italian opera-singers brought up on generations of gloomy, weather-torn sets for Donizetti's *Lucia di Lammermoor*, sweltered in Princes Street Gardens and swore blind that whatever might be the Scottish capital's Athenian pretensions, Edinburgh was definitely the Naples of the North.

Even after the clamorous success of the first Festival, Edinburgh citizens were not too sure about it. 'It couldn't have been us that did it,' they smirked at one another. 'It must have been a fluke.'

And, in a sense, they were right enough. The impetus for the Festival came largely from outside.

MAJOR FESTIVAL FOR BRITAIN
Rudolf Bing, then the manager of Glyndebourne Opera, wanted to create a major festival in Britain while the only two arts festivals in the world which counted for anything, Salzburg and Bayreuth were struggling to raise themselves like phoenixes from the shattered and smouldering ruins of the Third Reich. It was an act of calculated cultural banditry. Bing did not care where the festival was to be held. He tried first for Oxford and Cambridge, both convenient to the pool of culture enthusiasts centred in London and the home counties.

Edinburgh only came into his calculations when the great university cities of England showed little interest and when the persuasions of Audrey Christie, wife of Glyndebourne's founder, and H Harvey Wood, the British Council's man in Scotland, had advocated to him the virtues of the Scottish city.

Later Harvey Wood assembled some impressive, influential and persuasive Scottish patrons — among them Lady Rosebery, Lord Cameron and Sir Andrew Murray — to back the Festival idea and sell it to Edinburgh. Thanks to their support, the Lord Provost, Sir John Falconer, eloquently managed to persuade the City Fathers to vote money to set the Festival on its way.

Having no local composer — as Bayreuth has Wagner and Salzburg Mozart — around whom to build its festival, Edinburgh decided from the outset to 'go for broke', as the Americans say.

EDINBURGH MILITARY TATTOO

A feature of the Festival since 1947, the Tattoo takes place on the Esplanade of Edinburgh Castle. In this unrivalled setting soldiers march and counter march to the music of pipes and drums. Different visiting troops each year come from all over the world to take part in displays of service skills from drills and gymnastics to musical marches and dancing. Their often unusual forms of military dress add colour to the proceedings

MUSIC

From opera to folk and pop—all musical tastes are catered for during the Festival

PATTERN SET

In that first year of 1947, the operas *Le Nozze di Figaro* by Mozart and Verdi's *Macbeth* were given at the King's Theatre. At the Usher Hall there was the Vienna Philharmonic, reunited with Bruno Walter for the first time since he had been driven from Austria by Nazi persecution in 1937, and the Orchestre des Concerts Colonne from Paris.

There was also the Hallé under Barbirolli, the Liverpool Philharmonic under Sargent, the Scottish Orchestra under Susskind, the BBC Scottish Orchestra conducted by Ian Whyte and one of the most magical string quartets ever assembled, Schnabel, Szigeti, Fournier and Primrose.

At the Lyceum Theatre Louis Jouvet from Paris was playing Moliere's *L'École des Femmes* and Giraudoux's *Ondine* with Dominique Blanchar. The Old Vic staged *The Taming of the Shrew* with Trevor Howard, Bernard Miles and Patricia Burke and Alec Guinness's interpretation of *Richard II*.

At the Empire (now a bingo hall) Margot Fonteyn danced Tchaikovsky's *Sleeping Beauty* above the baton of Constant Lambert. At the Freemason's Hall there were morning chamber music concerts and recitals.

Other events such as exhibitions of painting and sculpture, the Tattoo and the enormous artistic splurge that is the Fringe were added later, but the basic festival pattern as it is today was established in 1947 — opera, concerts, chamber music, English and foreign language theatre and dance. The make-up and balance of the programme has varied with the tastes and interests of successive directors.

Bing departed after two years to be General Manager of the Metropolitan Opera in New York and he was succeeded by his 30-year-old assistant, Ian Hunter, a remarkable young man who had been a Lieutenant-Colonel during the war and created an opera company in occupied Austria.

Hunter added major art exhibitions — some of the greatest seen anywhere — and enlarged the opera spectrum by inviting foreign companies to perform.

Hunter left in 1956 and his successor, Robert Ponsonby continued the interest in the visual arts with memorable exhibitions of Braque and Monet, opera from La Scala, Milan and also some dazzling theatre from Italy directed by Giorgio Strehler. Among the ingredients Ponsonby introduced was satire — Anna Russell making fun of the Festival; Flanders and Swan pricking pomposities and most famous of all, *Beyond the Fringe* which introduced Dudley Moore, Peter Cook, Alan Bennett and Jonathan Miller to an appreciative world.

The Fringe itself was growing fast. In numbers of performances it had already outstripped the 'official' Festival. It included everything from biting satire, through one-man or woman shows to performances of the classics and chamber music.

These performances received no official financial backing and they were presented by amateurs, young professionals, university students and groups determined to make a name for themselves.

CULTIVATED INDISCIPLINE

The quality varied widely, as it still does today. The hectic, cultivated indiscipline of the Fringe regularly throws up performances of genius and tremendous talent and commitment and, just as regularly, rubbish and everything in between.

Nowadays, the only trouble about the Fringe is that by the time you have finished reading the massive programme, it is almost too late to go to anything! There can be anything up to 1000 titles, offered by 500 different companies plus exhibitions, 'happenings' and all kinds of music from pop to Stockhausen.

At Festival time, Fringe Festival, Film Festival, Jazz Festival, Book Festival and so on are presenting something like 300 performances a day. It is impossible to have a dull time in Edinburgh during the Festival.

There have been some stunningly memorable performances in the last forty years. Kathleen Ferrier's *Das Lied von der Erde,* with Bruno Walter; the rumbustious exuberance of the old Scots classic *The Thrie Estaites*; T S Eliot's *The Cocktail Party*; Jean-Louis Barrault's *Hamlet* in French; a great Verdi *Requiem* from the orchestra of La Scala; another *Hamlet* from Richard Burton and Claire Bloom; Maria Callas's *La Sonnambula* in the first decade.

When he became Director in 1961 Lord Harewood presented a superb performance of Schoenberg's *Gurrelieder* and featured particular composers in each year, notably Russians like Shostakovitch and Indian artists. Peter Diamand, the longest serving Festival Director, continued this plan and put the emphasis firmly back on great opera performances culminating in a magnificent *Carmen* with Berganza and Domingo, dazzlingly conducted by Claudio Abbado.

John Drummond, when he took over from Diamand in 1978, took another direction with more ballet performances, exhibitions and Russian drama.

Frank Dunlop, who took over in 1984, has mounted spectacular, wide-ranging world theatre with companies from Japan to Scandinavia.

The list of innovative and memorable performances threatens to stretch out, like Macbeth's line of kings 'to the crack of doom'.

And that is without taking account of the Fringe, which has grown more and more professional down the years, the Film Festival, the Jazz Festival, the Tattoo and many other events of these three hectic summer weeks!

There was a time when it was widely held that after the Festival the arts in Edinburgh died for 49 weeks. It was never true and today it is less true than ever.

Music is provided by regular concerts from the Scottish National Orchestra, the Scottish Chamber Orchestra, Scottish Baroque Ensemble, the Edinburgh Quartet and visiting groups and artists.

There is a very talented resident company at the Royal Lyceum Theatre and the Traverse in the Grassmarket remains a British leader in presenting new and avant-garde plays.

The City's fine museums and art galleries, the National Gallery, Royal Scottish Academy, the City Art Centre, the Scottish Gallery of Modern Art, Richard de Marco's new gallery in Blackfriars Street and the Fruitmarket Gallery offer constantly changing and challenging views of the visual arts.

There is folk music, rock and jazz in pubs, chamber music and recitals in the New Town and elsewhere throughout the year.

The arts flourish in Edinburgh all the year round. The Festival is simply the brilliant firework display which is the peak of the arts year in the capital of Scotland.

Iain Crawford

ART
The lover of modern art will not be disappointed as there are many Edinburgh galleries dedicated to the subject

FANTASTIC FINALE
In recent years, the last performance of the Tattoo has ended in a spectacular display of fireworks to the accompaniment of music by Handel

Famous residents

T o be a hero or a character in Edinburgh your deeds or your eccentricities should be on a very large scale, otherwise they stand in serious danger of being dwarfed by the city's dimension as landscape.

Yet that does not seem to have been a danger in the 18th-century days of Mr Amyat, King George's chemist:

Here I stand at what is called the cross of Edinburgh and can in a few minutes take 50 men of genius by the hand. . . . In Edinburgh the access to men of parts is not only easy but their conversation and the communication of their knowledge are at once imparted to intelligent strangers with the utmost liberality.

But there were characters in Edinburgh before Mr Amyat trod its streets, deemed heroes by some if less highly regarded by others.

George Heriot

JOHN KNOX — PROTESTANT REFORMER

One who was only too prepared to communicate his knowledge was John Knox, the famous Protestant reformer, challenger of Mary, Queen of Scots on her return to Scotland from France. Actually, it was Mary who challenged Knox.

She had returned to Scotland on the understanding that everyone should be allowed to practise religion in their own way. When she had mass said in the Chapel Royal, Knox thundered denunciation of her from the pulpit of St Giles High Kirk.

Mary summoned him to the Palace of Holyroodhouse, accusing him of treason and of insulting herself and her mother in writing his *First Blast of the Trumpet Against the Monstrous Regiment of Women*, published in 1558, in which he had asserted that the rule of women was 'the subversion of good order, of all equity and justice'.

In 1548 Knox had been captured at St Andrews Castle by the French and had spent two years as a galley slave on their ships, so he had no liking for French ways, which he associated with Mary. Knox brought to Scotland the austere doctrines of John Calvin with whom he had worked in Geneva. To a large degree his teachings set the pattern for Scottish religious and even social life over the next few centuries, not all of it harsh and over-moralistic, for it included wide-reaching provisions for democratic rule by elections and compulsory education.

JOHN KNOX
Despite his outbursts against women, John Knox was twice married, with five children. His formidable admonitory statue fronts the Assembly Hall

GOLD DIGGER AND MATHEMATICIAN — JOHN NAPIER

Born in Knox's lifetime in 1550 was John Napier of Merchiston, an Edinburgh man of very different stamp, son of the Master of the Scottish Mint who discovered gold in the Pentland Hills. He shared Knox's Presbyterian views but it was in the field of mathematics, astronomy and invention that he excelled.

Napier's supreme achievement was the invention of logarithms and the decimal point which led the way towards modern computer science. He also drew up plans for a tank, an armoured car, a submarine and a kind of death ray which used lenses to concentrate the sun's heat on the enemy.

His polymath ingenuity was used in more domestic episodes. He discovered that poultry were being stolen from his Merchiston estate and suspected his servants. Using his reputation as a man of magic, he told them he was going to discover the true thief by locking the suspects in a room with his magic black cockerel. Every man had to stroke the bird, he ordered, and at the thief's touch it would crow loudly.

In the darkened room, the black cockerel made the rounds and Napier waited. When light was restored, he examined the hands of all present and found only one man's hands without the soot he had smeared on the cockerel's feathers and the thief was unmasked.

The 15th-century tower in which Napier lived and worked is now the centrepiece of the college of advanced education named after him in Colinton Road. Napier College was opened in 1964, exactly 350 years after the publication of *Mirifici Logarithmorum Canonis Descriptio* — a fitting tribute to the man and his work.

FAME IN THE WORLD OF FINANCE

Just thirteen years younger than Napier was 'Jinglin' Geordie', George Heriot the goldsmith who became jeweller to James VI of Scotland and I of England and his consort, Anne of Denmark. Heriot is the most illustrious member of the Incorporation of Goldsmiths of the City of Edinburgh, which celebrated the tercentenary of its Royal Charter in 1987 and is the only guild in Scotland to have its own hallmark.

Jinglin' Geordie combined being the royal jeweller with the post of banker and moneylender to the royal family. When he died in London in 1623, he was a very rich man and his will made provisions for founding a children's home for the education and upbringing of orphans and fatherless children which has become George Heriot's School, built between 1628 and 1660, the finest Renaissance-style building in Edinburgh. There is also a pub named after him in Fleshmarket Close.

About this time the capital was gaining a reputation for influential bankers. William Paterson from Dumfriesshire founded the Bank of England in 1690 and was the prime mover in the disastrous Darien Scheme of 1698.

Before the Union of Parliaments in 1707, although they shared the same king, Scots were treated by the English as foreigners and debarred from trading with English colonies. In 1695, Paterson set up the Company of Scotland trading to Africa and the Indies as a proposed joint Scots and English company in London. The East India Company and other English traders vehemently opposed it and impeached its English founders for treachery. Scotland and its Parliament were furious and Paterson persuaded half Scotland to invest in a new project which would be for Scots alone, the Darien Scheme, a Scots colony in the Isthmus of Panama.

Unfortunately, the site was ill-chosen, its sovereignty challenged by Spain. The expedition which set out from Leith in 1698 to establish it was inexperienced and unhelped by the indifference, where it was not hostility, of the English colonists in America and the Caribbean. Two thousand lives and all the money and goods invested in its creation were lost and the project abandoned in 1700.

Paterson himself survived the Darien expedition and returned to Scotland to become an advocate of union with England, a move which he had done as much as anyone to achieve by bankrupting half his countrymen.

John Law, born in 1671, was another financial wizard, with a talent for tennis and gambling. After a series of adventures which included killing a man in a duel in London, being imprisoned and sentenced to death, travelling extensively on the Continent, and making money speculating in securities and foreign exchange in Italy, Holland and Switzerland, he returned to Edinburgh and settled in his family home, Lauriston Castle.

He tried to persuade the Scottish Parliament to improve the stricken economy by issuing banknotes but his suggestions were turned down and he set off again on his travels, to Brussels, Paris and his old haunt, Genoa, wheeling and dealing and writing works on political economy.

He offered his system for paying off the French National Debt to Louis XIV who rejected it on the somewhat illogical grounds that Law was not a Catholic.

A fervent advocate of bank-notes, he insisted that the secret of wealth for nations was 'to make gold out of paper' and in 1716 he set up a joint-stock bank with the connivance of the French Government and became a naturalised Frenchman. With the Company of the West he regulated and managed French trade with Louisiana and was responsible for founding the city of New Orleans. Honours were showered upon him. He was elected a member of the French Academy and is claimed to have been the first millionaire.

Adopting Henry of Navarre's dictum that 'Paris is worth a mass' he became a Roman Catholic and was appointed Controller-General of Finance to Louis XV and, although he was exiled after devaluation, he retired, apparently not too impoverished, to Venice where he died in 1729.

His family home, Lauriston Castle in Cramond Road North, is now owned by Edinburgh City and District Council.

JINGLIN' GEORDIE
George Heriot's unusual drinking cup—designed by 'Jinglin' Geordie' himself

ROBERT SIBBALD AND ANDREW BALFOUR

Edinburgh's Royal Botanical Gardens, among the finest in Europe, owe their creation to two 17th-century doctors, Robert Sibbald and Andrew Balfour, who planted medicinal herbs and plants in a Physic Garden near the Trinity Hospital in 1667. Over the years the garden was enlarged and extended in various locations in the New Town and moved to its present site in Inverleith in 1820.

A MUSICAL LEGACY

One of the few things to be said in favour of James VII and II is that while in Edinburgh as Duke of York and the King's Commissioner, in 1682 he instigated the first musical concerts in the tennis courts at Holyroodhouse.

St Cecilia's Hall, in the Cowgate, which is still used for concerts and recitals today was opened in 1762. As well as being used during the Edinburgh Festival and at other times, it houses the Russell Collection of keyboard instruments, including harpsichords, clavichords, chamber organs, spinets, virginals and fortepianos belonging to the Faculty of Music at Edinburgh University.

'Fiddler Tam', Thomas Erskine, the 6th Earl of Kellie was one of the prominent figures in Edinburgh's musical life of the time. A cheerful and boisterous character, renowned for his atrocious puns, he studied composition and the violin at Mannheim and wrote minuets for Edinburgh ladies which were popular south of the Border and on the Continent as well as in Scotland.

Another jolly figure, General John Reid, a Perthshire soldier who was a good flute player, left £52,000 in his will in 1807 to found a School of Music, still commemorated in the Reid Hall in the University. In 1841 the University made overtures to Felix Mendelssohn, who visited the city in 1829, to be the Reid Professor of Music, but Mendelssohn, busy in Leipzig and Berlin, politely declined.

SCOTLAND'S UNCROWNED KINGS

The 'men of genius' to be met in the High Street in the 18th century could have been painters, philosophers, writers, doctors, economists, engineers, sociologists architects, geologists, lawyers, ministers or explorers.

They might have included two men, each known in his time as 'the uncrowned king of Scotland', Duncan Forbes of Culloden, and Henry Dundas, 1st Viscount Melville.

As Lord President of the Court of Session, Forbes strove for justice tempered with mercy after the Jacobite

WILLIAM BURKE
Half of the legendary body-snatching duo Burke and Hare. He was hanged for strangling at least 16 paupers and selling the bodies for medical research

BRIDGE-BUILDER TO A NATION
Dean Bridge, in Dean Village, is a fine example of Thomas Telford's work

namesake's preoccupation with this cause, which among other things, saved the south side of Princes Street from being built upon.

POETS, THINKERS AND PIONEERS

There were poets galore — Robert Fergusson, whom Burns admired so much that he paid for his tombstone in Canongate Kirkyard; James Thomson who wrote *Rule Britannia*; Burns himself who was lionised in Edinburgh in 1786 and 1787; James Macpherson, the 'creator' of Ossian 'which ran like a flow of lava through Europe' according to Matthew Arnold. Macpherson was also praised by Schiller, Goethe, Ingres, Georges Sand, Mendelssohn and Brahms and adopted by Napoleon as his favourite poet.

Allan Ramsay the wigmaker, bookseller, playwright and poet lived here, as did his son of the same name, a distinguished portrait painter. Other local artists included Henry Raeburn and Alexander Nasmyth, famous as 'the father of Scottish landscape'.

Architects like Robert Adam and his family, played their part in changing the appearance of the city. Charlotte Square, Register House and the entrance to the University are the most important Adam buildings. Thomas Telford worked on the New Town as a stone mason and studied the making of roads and bridges.

David Hume, the genial empiricist was keeper of the Advocates' Library and entertained Rousseau, Dr Johnson and Benjamin Franklin. Hume's friend, Adam Smith, invented political economy with *The Wealth of Nations* in 1776.

Several famous explorers have associations with Edinburgh. James Bruce 'The Abyssinian', who discovered the source of the Blue Nile studied law at the University in the 1740s and Mungo Park, explorer of the Niger, read medicine in 1789. Alexander Gordon Laing, the first European to reach Timbuctoo was also an Edinburgh student.

The 19th century brought photography and two of its pioneers, David Octavius Hill and Robert Thomson, lived and worked in Edinburgh.

rebellion of 1745 against the kind of Hanoverian mentality exemplified by the Duke of Cumberland who called him 'that old woman who talked to me about humanity'. There is a superb statue by Roubiliac of Forbes laying down the law, beneath the hammer-beam roof of Parliament Hall in the High Street.

Henry Dundas stands on a pillar in the centre of St Andrew Square. He held several government offices under North and Pitt between 1777 and 1801 and survived impeachment in the House of Lords for his handling of the finances of the Navy.

He was widely known as Harry the Ninth. When Dundas was Home Secretary, that celebrated judge and diarist, Lord Cockburn said 'Henry Dundas, an Edinburgh man, and well calculated by talent and manner to make despotism popular, was the absolute dictator of Scotland and had the means of rewarding submission, and of supressing opposition, beyond what were ever exercised in modern times by one person, in any portion of the empire'.

THE COCKBURN ASSOCIATION

Henry Cockburn himself successfully defended the common-law wife of the bodysnatcher, Burke, and helped draft the Scottish Reform Bill. He loved life, good company and Edinburgh, and had a shrewd assessing eye for his fellow creatures, brilliantly demonstrated in his contributions to the *Edinburgh Review* and in *Memorials of His Time*.

The novelist, Evelyn Waugh and the journalist, Claud Cockburn are among his descendants and The Cockburn Association, concerned with the preservation and conservation of the best in Edinburgh, commemorates its

MEN OF LETTERS
*Two of Scotland's notable
literary geniuses, Sir
Walter Scott (top) and
Robert Louis Stevenson
(inset). An important
aspect of their lives in
common, and one which may
have contributed to their
writing talent, is that both
were sickly children who
spent many years in the
solitary confinement of their
bedrooms, and both turned
to reading as their favourite
pastime*

LITERARY GIANTS — SCOTT AND STEVENSON

Sir Walter Scott, although born in the 18th century (1771), became known as an author only in the 19th when he published a series of romantic epic poems under his own name and later wrote historical novels under the pseudonum 'Waverley'.

His novels had a profound influence all over the literate world and created an interest in Scotland which surpassed even Ossian. Scott's novels rival Shakespeare as source material for opera.

The other major Edinburgh literary figure is Robert Louis Stevenson, son of a family of lighthouse builders.

Much less of a sentimentalist than Scott, he was a more astringent writer as he proved in his macabre, schizophrenic novel, *The Strange Case of Dr Jekyll and Mr Hyde* (based on an Edinburgh character, Deacon Brodie, who was a respectable town councillor by day and a burglar by night), in his essays and in *The New Arabian Nights*. That he could also write gripping adventure yarns, he showed with *Treasure Island* and *Kidnapped*.

JAMES YOUNG SIMPSON
The relief of pain in surgery and childbirth owes much to this man's discovery of chloroform as an anaesthetic

MEDICINE AND MORE

Although Edinburgh had established a reputation as a medical centre earlier, it was in the 19th century that it really came to the fore.

James Lind had shown the way with his *Treatise on the Scurvy* in 1753 with which he demonstrated how scurvy could be prevented by the juice of citrus fruits. James Gregory, one of a brilliant scientific family, invented Gregory's Mixture, a universal pharmaceutical comforter used up to recent times.

James Syme, Edinburgh's Professor of Clinical Surgery, the greatest surgeon of his day, was known as 'the Napoleon of Surgery'.

James Young Simpson discovered the use of chloroform as an anaesthetic, was the first to use it in childbirth and founded modern practice in gynaecology.

James Lister was Syme's assistant and married his daughter. Eventually he succeeded Syme as Professor of Surgery. His work on antiseptics earned him a baronetcy and later he was the first doctor to be made a peer.

James Miranda Stuart Barry began studying medicine in Edinburgh at the age of ten, disguised as a boy. She served 46 years in the armed services before, as a result of having yellow fever, she was discovered to be a woman. Her secret was kept by the doctor who examined her and she rose to become Inspector-General of Military Hospitals in Canada.

Sir Arthur Conan Doyle was from an Edinburgh family, studied medicine in the city and served as a field surgeon in the Boer War. But his celebrity came from his Sherlock Holmes stories, the central character of which was based on the investigative capacities of Edinburgh surgeon, Dr Joseph Bell.

However, Edinburgh characters do not end with Conan Doyle and famous visitors to the city are more numerous than ever.

Among well-known names to whom Edinburgh was their first home are actors Sean Connery, Alistair Sim and Ronnie Corbett; broadcasters Magnus Magnusson, Ludovic Kennedy and Tom Fleming and composers Thea Musgrave and John Macleod.

There are many other names and you will not spend long in Scotland's capital before you have a few characters of your own to add to the historical list.

Iain Crawford

CITY CENTRE

TOWN·AND·CITY·GUIDES
AA
TOWN·AND·CITY·GUIDES

This ornate lantern can be seen above the entrance to the Palace of Holyroodhouse

BRIDGES IN EDINBURGH

An early concern of 18th-century Edinburgh planners was how to cross the wide valley (now occupied by Waverley Station) and join Old and New Town. The foundation stone of the first North Bridge was laid in 1763, though because of a partial collapse through faulty foundations, the project was not completed until 1772. Today's bridge is a reconstruction of 1897. The continuation of this main route south, known to generations as 'The Bridges', was carried by South Bridge, only really conspicuous as a bridge from the Cowgate below. It is a 19-arch construction dating from 1788.

The continuation of a roadway south from the Mound was by means of George IV Bridge, completed in 1836 and involving the wholesale destruction of a number of historic closes in the Royal Mile.

CAMERA OBSCURA AND OUTLOOK TOWER

Castle Hill
The lower storeys of this conspicuous building in Castlehill are 17th-century, while the upper floors with their 'castellations' were added around 1853 when an optician, Maria Theresa Short,

devised and built a camera obscura. With modifications over the years, this device still operates today, giving a panoramic view over the city.

In the 1890s, the property was acquired and the facilities expanded by Sir Patrick Geddes, the Edinburgh-born architect and town-planning pioneer. Today, the Outlook Tower is a visitor centre with exhibitions and displays as well as its still popular camera obscura.

CANONGATE CHURCH

Canongate
The Canongate Church dates from 1688 and is evidence of the formerly independent life of the burgh of Canongate. It was originally built for the congregation of the Abbey Church of Holyrood. The worshippers there were displaced when the Catholic King James VII of Scotland (II of England) ordered its conversion to a chapel for the Knights of the Thistle. Between 1946–53 Canongate Church was extensively restored and the Market Cross of the burgh was rebuilt in the churchyard. The poet, Robert Fergusson, the economist, Adam Smith and Robert Burns' 'Clarinda' are among some of the notable Scots buried there.

CANONGATE TOLBOOTH

Canongate
The Canongate Tolbooth was the civic centre of the burgh of Canongate, which had an independent status outside Edinburgh's town walls. Though there is evidence of a Tolbooth earlier than the late 15th century, the one surviving today was rebuilt in 1591 to include a Council Chamber. This was on the first floor, reached by the outside stairs. In 1840, a few years before the burgh merged with the city of Edinburgh, the Canongate Tolbooth's use as a council meeting place was discontinued. Between 1842–8 it was an overflow for the Calton Jail, before undergoing restoration in 1879. It is now another of the city's museums, with plans for exhibitions and displays on the history of trade unions and local history due for completion in 1988.

Even today, the handsome North (seen here from Calton Hill) and South Bridges form the major thoroughfare linking Princes Street and the New Town with all points south of the city

CHARLOTTE SQUARE

Widely held to be one of Europe's finest examples of civic architecture, Charlotte Square was planned in 1791 by Robert Adam, a year before his death. His brother, James, died in 1794 and, as a result, the original plan for symmetrical façades on the north and south sides was not rigidly followed. The palace-fronted north side, which commands attention as the finest part of the square, was built fairly closely to the original plan. On this north side are the official residence of the Secretary of State for Scotland, the headquarters of the National Trust for Scotland and the Trust's Georgian House.

CHURCHES IN EDINBURGH

Of Edinburgh's many churches, these are a few of the more notable near the city centre:

St Andrew's & St George's Church, *George Street* Of interest not only because of its fine design, but because its site in George Street was a second choice. Originally, it was intended for the east side of St Andrew Square, balancing St George's (now West Register House) on the west side of Charlotte Square—and in keeping with the overall symmetry of Craig's New Town plan. However, a wealthy and influential baronet, Sir Lawrence Dundas, procured, by dubious means, the site for his own mansion. This still stands as the headquarters of the Royal Bank of Scotland, while St Andrew's was relegated to nearby George Street.

St Cuthbert's Church, *Lothian Road* Built on the ancient site of the Culdee Church of St Cuthbert dating from the 8th century, this religious building has seen much rebuilding. It was damaged during a siege of the Castle in 1689, rebuilt in 1775 and again in 1892. Almost all of Edinburgh was in its parish till 1834. Its graveyard has an interesting watchtower. Nearby is St John's Church, a Gothic Revival building of 1816.

St Mary's Cathedral, *Palmerston Place* A comparatively late arrival to the Edinburgh skyline, St Mary's Cathedral is impressively seen along the length of Melville Street near the West End. Its foundations were laid in 1874 and its spires only added in 1917. It is said to be the largest ecclesiastical building constructed in Scotland since the Reformation.

St Stephen's Church, *St Vincent Street* Prominent at the foot of Howe Street and conspicuous from Frederick Street above, this large church is said to have been built in 1826 by the city authorities deliberately to block the view of the handsome façade of Edinburgh Academy, immediately behind it and erected three years before. This uncharitable gesture apparently resulted from the Edinburgh Academy's opening as a privately-funded rival to the Town Council's own Royal High School!

CITY ART CENTRE

Market Street
A handsome, former warehouse, originally intended to store newsprint for *The Scotsman* newspaper next door, is now the home of Edinburgh's own fine art collection. This collection comprises about 3,000 paintings, drawings, prints and sculptures, mostly by Scottish artists, from the 17th century to the present. Views of Edinburgh, portraits of its famous citizens and other items of historical significance are also well represented and there is a wide-ranging exhibition programme.

Opposite is the Fruitmarket Gallery, likewise in a converted warehouse, which also offers a varied programme, concentrating mainly on contemporary Scottish and international fine art.

Charlotte Square—all the elegance of a bygone era. Inset: Local art through the ages is the main subject at the City Art Centre

CALTON HILL

At just over 350ft (110m) Edinburgh's Calton Hill is hardly a dominating height, yet it stands conspicuously on a sight-line along Princes Street and commands attention by the extraordinary architecture scattered across its domed top. It also looks particularly striking from Salisbury Crags in Holyrood Park, when the impressive façade of the former Royal High School, strung along the base of the hill, echoes the columns of the monuments on top. Equally eye-catching is the completely different aspect from Ferry Road to the north near Goldenacre, with Arthur's Seat itself providing an imposing background.

It is probably the best place for a city view with the minimum of effort. Visitors can walk up a steep, stepped path from Waterloo Place, the continuation of Princes Street, or drive up a curving road which starts just before the former Royal High School. The hill was said to be one of the favourite viewpoints of Robert Louis Stevenson, a writer

who knew the area well. (His cousins lived in nearby Royal Terrace and, as a child, Stevenson often played in the adjacent gardens.)

In Stevenson's time, the hill would have presented much the same appearance as it does today. Its extravagant collection dates mainly from the latter half of the 18th century and into the first three decades of the 19th century, when a great enthusiasm for neo-classicism gripped the city and its architects. The columns and temples of Calton Hill certainly helped Edinburgh earn its reputation as 'the Athens of the north'.

The strange unfinished grandeur of the National Monument is the hill's most conspicuous feature. Designed by Playfair, it was intended to be a model of the Parthenon on the Acropolis in Athens and a monument to the dead of the Napoleonic Wars. The foundation stone was laid in 1822, but by 1830 money had run out. The 12 pillars of locally-quarried stone now stand as a monument to high hopes but unsuccessful fund-raising. Though they have earned such titles as 'Edinburgh's Disgrace' and

'Scotland's Pride and Poverty' they contribute greatly to the drama of the city skyline.

The earliest building on the hill is the Old Observatory of 1766. This was designed by James Craig, the designer of the competition-winning street layout of the original New Town. By contrast, Craig's Old Observatory forsakes neo-classical preoccupations and is instead in a Gothic style, with little castellations. Before astronomical observations were moved to Blackford Hill, a New Observatory was built, this time designed by the prolific Playfair in 1818. It is easily identified as the conspicuous cross-shaped temple. Visitors encounter the architect again in the less imposing Playfair Monument, noted as part of the Observatory perimeter wall. This was to the architect's uncle, John Playfair, mathematician and natural philosopher, who was influential in the building of the Observatory in the first place.

Panoramic view of the city from Calton Hill with the Dugald Stewart Memorial in the foreground. Inset left: The Nelson Monument. Insert right: The Old Observatory

The visitor has yet more Playfair to note. He designed the circular little hilltop temple in 1830 as a monument to Dugald Stewart, one-time Professor of Moral Philosophy. It was inspired by the Lysicrates Monument from 4th-century Athens—clearly a very inspiring piece, as it was also used as a model for the monument to Robert Burns on Regent Road below, this time by Thomas Hamilton in 1830.

One more conspicuous monument catches the visitor's eye. This is the Nelson Monument, its upturned telescope shape entirely appropriate and designed by Robert Burn (not to be confused with the poet, but the father of the better-known architect, William). Built in 1816, the Nelson Monument has a time-ball on top—a device which, after being hoisted up by machinery, drops on the stroke of one o'clock. It is said to have been originally intended as a time-check for sailors in the port of Leith.

Calton Hill offers almost a complete panorama, with only the bulk of Arthur's Seat interrupting the views to distant horizons. The Lomond Hills of Fife are visible across the Forth in one direction, while in the other, the Pentlands can be seen beyond the spire of St Giles. To the east, along the crescent shape of the East Lothian coastline, the Berwick Law and the Bass Rock are visible. Like Arthur's Seat and the Calton Hill itself, they are volcanic in origin.

Among the nearer landmarks close by the hill is the Old Calton Burial Ground, divided in two in 1815 by the opening of Waterloo Place, with the Regent Bridge joining Princes Street to the flanks of the Calton Hill. The prominent obelisk is the Martyrs' Monument, designed by Thomas Hamilton in 1844 to commemorate political martyrs of 1793. Also in the Old Burial Ground are a number of other monuments, including one to David Hume, the philosopher, by Robert Adam (1777).

The comparatively modern St Andrew's House (1937), on the southern flanks of the hill, east of the Old Burial Ground, was built on the site of the Calton Jail. The Governor's House with its comic battlements has survived and perches above the steep slopes overlooking Waverley Station.

The trees immediately to the east are in the gardens of Royal Terrace, which along with Calton Terrace and Regent Terrace make up a late phase of New Town building. The north-facing Royal Terrace is the longest continuous neo-classical frontage to be found anywhere in Edinburgh. It was intended to overlook a further stately development running down to the sea at Leith—though as the visitor will readily note from the Calton Hill vantage point, this other grand New Town was never built.

CITY CHAMBERS

Royal Mile
The City Chambers were completed in 1761 and were thus a very early development in the great wave of new building which resulted in Edinburgh's New Town to the north. Though the frontage as seen from the High Street is impressive, the rear of the building rises a spectacular 12 storeys from Cockburn Street.

The building was originally conceived as the Royal Exchange—a place where merchants, lawyers and other branches of commerce could meet for business. During its construction, excavated material was taken up the Royal Mile and used as foundations for the Castle Esplanade. However, as a commercial venue the Royal Exchange was not successful and was taken over by the Town Council in 1811. Shops lingered on in the forecourt and in the arches until the end of the century.

COLINTON

A former milling village, Colinton bridges the gap between town and country with its wooded walkway along the banks of the Water of Leith. Particularly picturesque in autumn, the path partly utilises the now-vanished railway branch line which, when it opened, helped make this village 'desirable' to wealthy commuters. The local parish church of 1771 was once the ministry of the Reverend Dr Lewis Balfour, maternal grandfather of the writer, Robert Louis Stevenson, and often visited by him as a boy. The author recalls in an essay many details of the church and manse which can still be seen today.

CORSTORPHINE

Now a suburb of the city, the former village of Corstorphine was once separated from it by a loch and marsh to the west of the Water of Leith. Travellers were guided across the marshes by a lamp in the tower of Corstorphine Church (now a symbolic electric lamp). No trace remains of Corstorphine Castle except for some fine old trees and a well-preserved doo'cot (dovecote) on the former estate. As well as the old village's farming interests it once had a sulphurous spring which gained it minor prominence as a spa resort. It had lost both its spring and its loch by the 1830s. Corstorphine is also the home of the Edinburgh Tapestry Company, founded by the son of William Morris in 1910.

CRAIGMILLAR CASTLE

Though more than a little overshadowed by Edinburgh Castle, and in less attractive surroundings from the visitor's viewpoint, Craigmillar Castle (AM) is, nevertheless, a fine example of a fortified baronial house. It is also of considerable historic significance. Mary, Queen of Scots retreated here after the murder of Rizzo. The plot for the murder of her second husband, Darnley, was also hatched here. The castle itself was captured and burned by the Earl of Hertford in 1544.

Originally in the hands of the Preston family, who built the central L-plan tower in 1374, the castle was strengthened in 1427 with curtain walls all around. Further defences were added after Hertford's raid and later rebuilding took place in the 17th century.

CRAMOND

Known as *Alaterva* to the Romans, Cramond, at the mouth of the little River Almond, was once a port used while the Antonine Wall was under construction further up the Forth. Later developments all but destroyed a Roman fort here, though a variety of Roman artefacts have been uncovered nearby. Further upstream is evidence of its later industrial role as a once-thriving ironworks, with water-powered mills. Still visible are the remains of the small docks into which vessels took coal and ores and left with steel and wrought iron. This activity was at a peak in the 18th century. The remains of some of the mills can be seen in the pleasant leafy walk upstream. Today, visitors come to enjoy the views across the Firth of Forth, the pleasant environs of the neat, white-washed cottages and to admire the yachts of the local club.

An old mort safe, used to deter body-snatchers, can still be seen to the left of the entrance to Colinton churchyard.

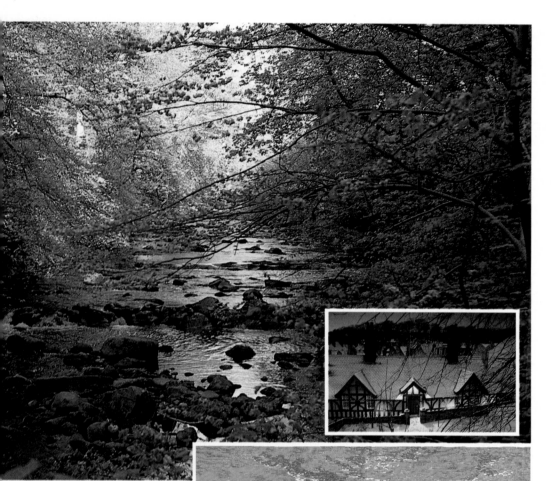

*The Water of Leith offers a leafy glade
in the centre of the city. Inset: Dean
Village—like a scene from a Christmas
card. Right: Duddingston Loch*

DEAN VILLAGE

One of Edinburgh's surprises is the
environs of this former milling
community on the banks of the
Water of Leith only a few minutes'
walk from Princes Street. No mills
now operate, but the work of the
Baxters (bakers) with their trade
guild is recalled in several existing
features such as their badge cut in
the stonework of the narrow bridge
over the Water of Leith.

This bridge and the steep road
down, Bell's Brae, were formerly the
main route out of Edinburgh to the
north until the building of the Dean
Bridge by Telford (1832) which still
carries today's traffic. Though
overshadowed and bypassed, the
little village should not be
overlooked. Visitors can join the
Water of Leith walkway here.
Downstream, the pathway leaves
the village, passes under the Dean
Bridge, goes past St Bernard's Well
and emerges at Stockbridge.

DUDDINGSTON

Tucked beyond the bulk of Arthur's
Seat, the once isolated village of
Duddingston, formerly a weaving
community, reveals its antiquity in a
number of interesting features. The
most conspicuous of these is its
church, Norman in origin. Though
greatly altered, its richly carved
doorway remains. Its churchyard
still has a watchtower to guard
against bodysnatchers, while at the
gate of the church a pair of 'jougs'
survive. These consist of an iron
collar, attached to the wall by a
chain. Wrongdoers were clamped
into it in full view. Also close by is a
'loupin' on stane' or mounting
block.

The ancient Sheep's Heid Inn is
found in the village and claims the
oldest skittle alley in Scotland.
Nearby is Duddingston Loch, a bird
sanctuary since 1923, now in the
care of the Scottish Wildlife Trust.

EDINBURGH CASTLE

The shape of the Castle Rock is the result of an eastward moving glacier scouring round the hard volcanic rock to form three steep sides and a long ramp pointing east. This formed the Royal Mile. The process is called a 'crag and tail' by geologists. The crag became the Castle Rock, while the tail slopes down to Holyrood. Inevitably, with such strong defensive possibilities, the site has been occupied since the very earliest times, probably originally by Iron Age peoples. The Romans, however, seemed to have built their main fortifications elsewhere. Picts and Saxons in an early power-struggle may each have occupied the site, but by the 7th century Edwin of Northumbria had built a castle. In the 10th century the Castle Rock was part of the kingdom of Alba and became thoroughly Scottish after King Malcolm defeated the Northumbrians in 1018. Thereafter, facts become more easily separated from early legend. Malcolm's wife, the saintly Queen Margaret, died in the Castle in 1093. She had been instrumental in persuading King Malcolm to move the royal court from Dunfermline to Edinburgh.

Her chapel still survives on the highest point of the Castle Rock and, though greatly rebuilt, remains as one of Scotland's oldest ecclesiastical buildings. Little else has survived from those early days. The tumult of wars and sieges right down to the Jacobite rebellions in the 18th century have inevitably wrought great changes in the appearance of the Castle.

For example, its Esplanade, the grand setting of the spectacular Military Tattoo, was built in 1753 with material excavated during the building of the Royal Exchange. Before that, the approach to the Castle had been much steeper. Similarly, the Gatehouse is a Victorian addition, with the statues of Robert the Bruce and William Wallace, two of Scotland's greatest heroes, placed on guard there only in 1929, during the celebrations to mark the city's 600th anniversary as a Royal Burgh. The Portcullis Gate

beyond is on the site of the Constable's Tower, destroyed during 1573 when Kirkcaldy of Grange held the Castle for Mary, Queen of Scots.

This particularly destructive incident also resulted in the building of the conspicuous Half-Moon Battery, erected just after the successful siege by the Regent Morton. Again, it was built on a fortification destroyed by cannon—David's Tower of 1367, which had withstood the forces of the English Kings Richard II in 1385 and Henry IV in 1400. The firepower of the Half-Moon Battery overlooks the houses of the Old Town and was unpopular with the early citizens.

The Castle's last siege was during the 1745 Rebellion. While Bonnie Prince Charlie enjoyed himself in the Palace of Holyroodhouse, at the other end of the Royal Mile the Castle's garrison held out for the Hanoverian government. At the end of October, an unknown soldier must have fired the last shot in anger as the Prince and his forces rode out

of town—and the Castle's strategic role in military conflict came to an end.

The Castle still has a substantial military presence, including the headquarters of the Royal Scots and the Royal Scots Dragoon Guards. Some of the buildings, including office and mess accommodation, are not open to public inspection. Visitors can trace much military history in the nearby United Services Museum, founded in 1933, which contains many relics. Also notable is the Scottish National War Memorial, designed by Sir Robert Lorimer and opened in 1927. It is built on the site of the Castle's own church. There are plenty of other places of interest for the visitor to see on the Castle Rock, including the Great Hall, built by James IV in the early 16th century, though somewhat over-restored since. It housed the Scottish Parliament before Parliament House was built. The need to find a level space for the Great Hall resulted in great vaults being built beneath. They have become known as the French

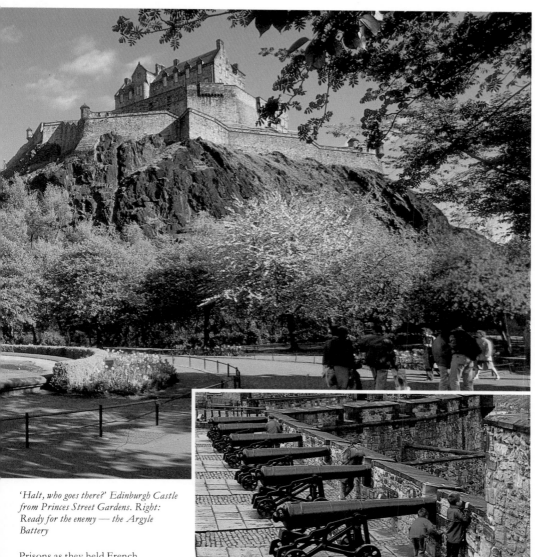

'Halt, who goes there?' Edinburgh Castle from Princes Street Gardens. Right: Ready for the enemy — the Argyle Battery

Prisons as they held French prisoners of war during the Napoleonic Wars. Graffiti written by their French occupants can still be seen.

Also below ground and protected from the weather is the famous Mons Meg, now in the vaults. This 15th-century cannon has a variety of explanations of its origins, but what is known is that it burst during the firing of a salute to the Duke of York in 1682 and lay derelict before it was taken to the Tower of London in 1754. Through the influence of Sir Walter Scott it was returned to the Castle in 1829.

Sir Walter was responsible for the recovery of even more important Scottish artefacts. The Scottish crown, sceptre and sword of state, the Regalia of Scotland, were locked away in a trunk in 1707 at the Union of the Crowns. They lay dusty and forgotten until Scott obtained

permission from the King in distant London to search for them. Now they are on display in the Crown Room, which is part of the Palace and King's Lodging on one side of the Crown Square. The name of this building is a reminder that it was the royal residence in Edinburgh until the completion of Holyrood. Also within are Queen Mary's Rooms, including Mary's bedroom where King James VI of Scotland (I of England) was born. Initials of mother and son adorn the roof panels and the monogram of Mary and Lord Darnley can be seen above the entrance doorway to her rooms.

One of the most obvious customs connected with the Castle may cause momentary alarm to casual visitors

strolling in Princes Street or its gardens. The firing of the One o' Clock Gun on weekdays dates back to 1848 and its unexpectedly loud report echoes round the streets of the New Town. Since 1861 it has been connected electrically to the fall of a time-ball seen on top of the Nelson Monument on Calton Hill— just one of the city's landmarks which can be seen from the Castle ramparts. With the unmistakable outline of the Castle adding so much to Edinburgh's unique skyline— particularly when floodlit on a summer evening—it is hardly surprising that this high vantage point offers superb views, as far as hills such as Ben Ledi and Ben Vorlich beyond the Highland line.

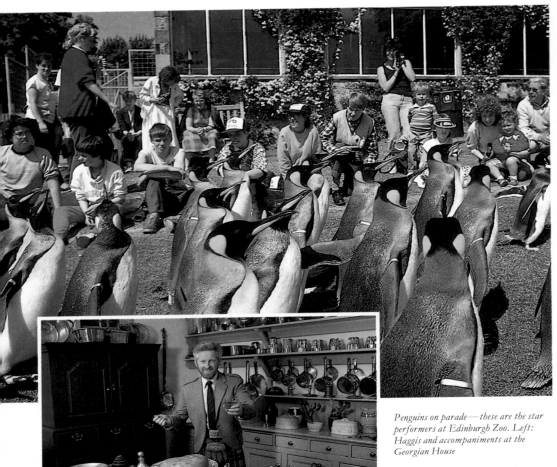

Penguins on parade—these are the star performers at Edinburgh Zoo. Left: Haggis and accompaniments at the Georgian House

EDINBURGH ZOO

On the south-facing slopes of Corstorphine Hill is the Royal Zoological Society of Scotland's Edinburgh Zoo, covering 70 acres. It was founded in 1913. Its most famous exhibit is its colony of both king and gentoo penguins, which take their famous walk, the 'Penguin Parade', round part of the zoo every day during the summer months.

GEORGE HERIOT'S SCHOOL

George Heriot had a tiny workshop along the north side of St Giles, in the line of booths known as the krames, which survived until 1817. More importantly, he was also goldsmith to King James VI. Through his gold and jewellery trade, 'Jinglin' Geordie' amassed a fortune and arranged through a trust that it was used to create a 'hospital for the maintenance, relief, bringing-up and educating poor fatherless boys . . .'

Heriot died in 1623; his hospital/school was duly built by 1650, promptly occupied by Cromwell's sick and injured troops for the next eight years, then received its first pupils in the following year. The Heriot Trust went on to open other schools and George Heriot's Hospital was renamed George Heriot's School in 1886. It remains today, south of the Grassmarket, and its distinctive turrets can be seen from the Castle.

THE GEORGIAN HOUSE

Charlotte Square
Part of the magnificent façade on the north side of Charlotte Square, No. 7 has been restored by the National Trust of Scotland. It recreates, down to the finest detail, a Georgian town house of around 1800, that is, when the building was new and in the very height of fashion. Furniture, fabrics and décor are correct for the period and provide a fascinating insight into the customs and lifestyle of the times, not only in the elegant public rooms, but in the labour-intensive kitchen below stairs.

GLADSTONE'S LAND

Castle Hill
This six-storey tenement on the Lawnmarket preserves its original arcaded front of around 1631—a unique survival of a feature once common in Scottish domestic architecture. It was built by a merchant, Thomas Gledstanes, who rebuilt an even earlier structure, traces of which are still visible inside the building today. Today's visitors can also see unusual original ceiling and wall paintings and original fireplaces. The building was acquired by the National Trust for Scotland in 1934 and is now renovated and refurbished as a typical house of a 17th-century merchant.

GRASSMARKET

King James III of Scotland granted a charter to hold markets in the Grassmarket in 1477. Though just south of the castle, at that time the area still lay outside the town walls. Later it was contained by the Flodden Wall of 1514–60. The main road from the west ran through the Grassmarket, entering by the West Port, a name which survives today. Though a place of commerce through the centuries, it was also the scene of many hangings. The gallows' site is marked today by railings and a rose-coloured cross set into the cobble-stones. Among the surviving buildings is the White Hart Inn, where Robert Burns and, later, William Wordsworth stayed on their visits to the city.

Originally, to reach the Castle via the Lawnmarket, the traveller had to go up the West Bow, which twisted steeply up from the east end of the Grassmarket, but the Victorian development of Victoria Street cut through this old thoroughfare. Now the Grassmarket end of the West Bow leads into Victoria Street, while the top end, the Upper Bow, can still be found leading off the Lawnmarket, connected to the lower level by a flight of steps. Victoria Street itself is an interesting shopping street, with a fine variety of craft, antique, print and other unusual shops.

GREYFRIARS BOBBY

Greyfriars Bobby was a Skye terrier who was devoted to his master, a local police constable, John Gray. After his master's death in 1858, the dog lingered near his grave in Greyfriars Churchyard for 14 years. In doing so he became a local celebrity, going daily to be fed at a nearby restaurant on hearing the one o'clock gun! (This was probably good for business.) So popular was the faithful Bobby that the Lord Provost himself paid for his licence. The dog so moved the citizens of Edinburgh that in 1873 a bronze statue, by William Brodie, was erected to the faithful animal. To this day it stands near the churchyard, on the junction of Candlemaker Row and George IV Bridge. Items associated with Bobby, including his collar and dish, are preserved in Huntly House Museum.

Greyfriars Bobby, the faithful Skye terrier

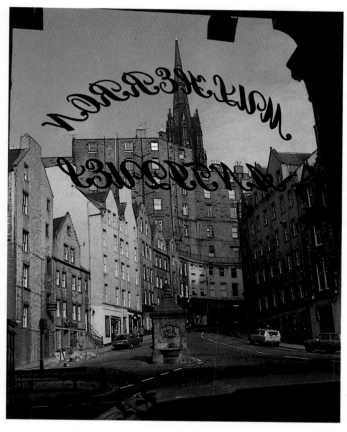

GREYFRIARS CHURCH

Along with its churchyard, this church occupies the site of an earlier Franciscan monastery. It played an important part in Scottish religious history as the place where the National Covenant was signed in 1638, which plunged the nation soon after into drawn-out religious wars.

About 1,200 Covenanters, captured at the Battle of Bothwell Brig in 1679, were held here without shelter for five months, while other martyrs to the Covenanters' cause are commemorated in memorials within the walls.

Greyfriars Church itself first opened for worship in 1620, was desecrated by Cromwell's troops in 1650, had a New Church built and attached to its west end in 1721, burned down in 1845 and later restored.

In a dramatic sweeping curve of high tenements and interesting shops, Victoria Street meets the Grassmarket

HEART OF MIDLOTHIAN

High Street
Look for the cobbled stones set in a heart-shape on the High Street between St Giles and George IV Bridge. This marks the spot of the Old Tolbooth, latterly the town prison, demolished in 1817. The outline of the building is also marked on the road with brass plates. It is remembered as the Heart of Midlothian following the description of it in Sir Walter Scott's novel of the same name.

HILLEND SKI CENTRE

Fairmilehead
Beyond the suburb of Fairmilehead on the north-facing slope of the Pentland Hills is the Hillend Ski Centre, with the longest artificial ski slope in Britain, dropping from around 1,200ft (370m) and popular throughout the year. Its chairlift offers non-skiers easy access to the Pentland Hills and magnificent views across the city and the Firth of Forth to Fife and beyond.

Salisbury Crags and Holyrood Park.
Inset: High above the city, the man-made
Dunsappie Loch plays host to hundreds
of water-birds

HOLYROOD PARK & ARTHUR'S SEAT

The rough slopes of Arthur's Seat would be a scenic asset in any part of Scotland. That they are a few minutes from Edinburgh's city centre is a bonus for visitors and residents alike. They provide an easy escape into the countryside, interest for the geologist and naturalist and fine views for everyone from many parts of this royal park. Formerly the King's or Queen's Park, it was first enclosed by King James V as a preserve for royal game.

Its highest point is the summit of Arthur's Seat, 822ft (253m) high. Its distinctive shape owes much to its volcanic origin about 235 million years ago. The summit, the so-called 'Lion's Head', along with the lower 'Lion's Haunch' were two volcanic vents, the more rounded Whinny Hill to the east was the volcanic cone with its stepped lava ridges. The formations were subsequently tilted by major earth movements and later molten rock pushed through the strata to form, after much erosion, the sill of Salisbury Crags.

A number of factors have resulted in its present appearance. These include generations of grazing, now closely controlled, the insensitive quarrying of Salisbury Crags—which a series of law-suits between 1819 and 31 finally stopped—and the building of the Radical Road. Sir Walter Scott is credited with the

original idea for this project—a roadway, built in 1820 which encircles the park at high level. The road recalls the radical views of the weavers and other tradesmen who were employed in this early 'job-creation' scheme. Both Dunsapie, high on the hill, and St Margaret's Lochs are artificial, created last century by damming and drainage. Visitors should note that there is also a one-way drive, which shortens the climb to the top of Arthur's Seat.

Though traces of early settlement have been found in the past, and the park was the site of several hilltop forts, the stones have long since been removed. Early cultivation terraces are noticeable on the east side of the hill, particularly when lit by a low sun. Much later are the remains of St Anthony's Chapel, overlooking St Margaret's Loch. It dates from around 1430 and fell into disuse at the time of the Reformation. Also of interest, on the north side of Salisbury Crags near Holyrood Palace, is St Margaret's Well, moved in 1862 from Restalrig, as it was in the way

of developments on the North British Railway.

There are numerous walks for visitors in the park. The summit can be reached from the Queen's Drive, or from near St Anthony's Chapel. There is a footpath running high along the base of Salisbury Crags—and another route along the cliff tops. Visitors wandering on Whinny Hill can lose sight of the city entirely, as they can also in Hunter's Bog, at the foot of the long dip slope behind Salisbury Crags. Botanists will look out for such unusual plants as Red German Catchfly and Maiden Pink, while birdwatchers will enjoy a wide variety of species particularly around Duddingston Loch. Visitors interested in geology should note the protected sites in the old quarries on the crags, as well as Samson's Ribs—conspicuous dolerite columns on the cliff-face, seen clearly from the Queen's Drive on the way to Duddingston. Full details of the natural history of the park can be found in the Scottish Wildlife Trust's Visitor Centre, near the Palace gates.

HUNTLY HOUSE

Canongate

One of the best-preserved 16th-century buildings in the Old Town, Huntly House, overlooking the Canongate, was rebuilt in 1570 from earlier work. In the 18th century it became the headquarters of one of the city's guilds, the Hammermen (smiths) of the Canongate. In 1924 it was bought by the city and later became the most important museum of local history, with a wide-ranging collection including silver, glassware, pottery, shop signs and other trade artefacts as well as many relics from other demolished buildings.

Its name recalls an association with the first Marquess of Huntly, who is supposed to have lived there in the 16th century, though not all historians agree on this point.

JOHN KNOX HOUSE

High Street

This is a fine example of pre-Reformation domestic architecture dating from around the beginning of the 16th century. Some historians doubt that John Knox himself actually ever lived in it—though it is certainly old enough. Nevertheless, it was only a strongly-held belief that he died there in 1572 that preserved the building when it was about to be demolished in 1849.

Its projecting gallery at first-floor level is the only surviving example of what was once a common feature in Edinburgh's High Street. The initials inscribed on the outside are those of James Mossman (and his wife), goldsmith to Mary, Queen of Scots. Today, the house is a museum which includes painted panelling discovered in a recent restoration.

Lady Stair's House, now a literary museum

Models in regimental dress can be seen in Huntly House, principal museum of local history. Inset: Attractive gardens surround Lauriston House

LADY STAIR'S HOUSE

Bank Street

This town house of 1622 is the only surviving building of the original Lady Stair's Close. At one stage in the late 18th century, the close became the main route connecting the nearby Lawnmarket—part of the Royal Mile—with the developing New Town via the Mound. Earlier, the house itself was owned by the widow of the first Earl of Stair, Lady Stair, who died in 1759.

The building was bought by Lord Rosebery in 1895 and presented to the city in 1907. It is currently a museum containing artefacts associated with the lives of three famous literary Scots: Robert Louis Stevenson, Sir Walter Scott and Robert Burns.

LAURISTON CASTLE

Cramond Road South

This intriguing example of the Edwardian age is held in trust by the City of Edinburgh. The tower house of 1590, with its extensive Jacobean extension by William Burn in 1827, and later library, still retains the atmosphere of a gracious country mansion. The peaceful grounds offer pleasant walks overlooking the Firth of Forth near Cramond and its extensive lawns are used by the Edinburgh Croquet Club.

Today's visitors can enjoy the conservative Edwardian interiors with their period furniture, Derbyshire Blue John ornaments, Crossley wool 'mosaics' and minor *objets d'art*.

LEITH

The ancient seaport of the capital, Leith lost its independent status as recently as 1920—though it had only gained it in 1833. A few incidents from its turbulent past include the arrival by sea of many famous figures in Scottish history, including most of the Stuart monarchs—Mary, Queen of Scots arrived in 1561. The previous year the port had been besieged in battles between French Catholic troops under Mary's mother, Mary of Guise, and Protestant forces. It was occupied by Cromwell's troops in 1650. George IV disembarked at Leith in 1822.

The townsfolk once enjoyed golf on its still-surviving links and horse-racing on its sands. The Honourable Company of Edinburgh Golfers, one of the very first golf clubs, built premises in Leith in 1768. Nevertheless, the town has been predominantly a commercial port and, until recently, recession, decline of traditional local industries and insensitive redevelopment took their toll. Now, a new consciousness of Leith's heritage has awakened and the area is becoming distinctly fashionable. Commercial, civic and domestic architecture has been extensively refurbished and Leith now offers nightlife in restaurants and bars to match anything available anywhere near Princes Street.

MALLENY GARDENS

Balerno
In Balerno, on the outskirts of the city, the garden is laid out around a 17th-century house (not on view) built for Sir James Murray of Kilbaberton. It offers an interesting woodland walk and a good collection of shrub roses.

MEADOWBANK SPORTS CENTRE

Only a few minutes from the city centre, Edinburgh's major sports complex, originally built for the Commonwealth Games of 1970, includes a 15,000-seat stadium (8,000 covered). It offers a wide range of facilities and a temporary membership scheme for visitors.

THE MEADOWS

This tree-studded parkland, now used for sports, funfairs, festivals and other recreation, was once a loch, the South or Borough Loch, finally drained in 1740. It was the

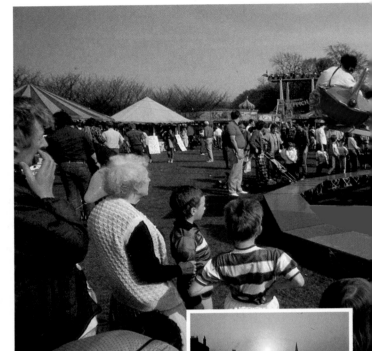

The Meadows—a downtown playground for Edinburgh folk. Right: Sunset over the Water of Leith

scene of the first British international exhibition held outside London—the International Exhibition of Industry, Science and Art, staged in 1886. Two and a half million people visited the event, which had 7 acres of buildings, including a Grand Hall with seating for 10,000. Unfortunately the builders had not reckoned on an Act of Parliament which vetoed building on the Meadows—everything, including the hall, had to be demolished immediately the exhibition finished!

Today's visitors should look for the pillars at the western end of Melville Drive, erected by the local stonemason's guild, the sundial commemorating the exhibition opening by Prince Albert and the whalebones on Jawbone Walk, presented by the Zetland Fair Isle Knitting Stand!

Adjacent to the south is Bruntsfield Links, more undulating parkland, and site of one of the city's very earliest golf courses, dating from around 1695, though records go back a century earlier, with the Bruntsfield Links Golfing Society dating from 1761. Since 1890 a short-hole pitch and putt course has been in existence here.

THE MOUND

An 18th-century Edinburgh tailor, George Boyd, was the first to see the need for an easy crossing between the Old Town, running down from

the Castle, and the blossoming New Town to the north. Between them lay the muddy quagmire of the former Nor' Loch, then in the process of being drained—Princes Street Gardens and the railway occupy the site today.

Anxious to give his New Town customers an easy passage to his Old Town shop, Boyd and some neighbours began making their own rough causeway. This project was taken up by the city authorities and orders were given for the construction of a huge ramp, made from the excavated material from the New Town building programme which was dumped on the site. When completed in 1830, it was estimated that the Mound contained over two million cartloads! First the Royal Scottish Academy, then the National Gallery were built to enhance the lower end of the Mound, while the top still gives a fine view over Princes Street. 'Geordie Boyd's Mud Brig' remains a vital link between the Old and the New.

MUSEUM OF CHILDHOOD

High Street
One of Edinburgh's most attractive museums, the unique Museum of Childhood in the High Street fascinates visitors of all ages. In 1986 it re-opened after major alteration and expansion which doubled its display area and now includes a restored Georgian Theatre. Toys, dolls, games and all the paraphernalia of childhood through the ages have made this museum internationally famous.

NATIONAL GALLERY OF SCOTLAND

The Mound
One of two fine neo-classical buildings by Playfair on the Mound, the National Gallery is one of Europe's finest smaller galleries with a distinguished collection of Old Masters, Impressionist and Scottish paintings. In addition to the two main viewing areas, with the Scottish collection mainly in the new wing, below ground level, there is a library and facilities for viewing works within the collection not on public display.

The architect William Playfair's earlier work, now the Royal Scottish Academy, is adjacent to the National Gallery, on the Princes Street end of the Mound, and mounts its own exhibition annually.

Light and space are used to maximum effect in the Royal Scottish Museum in Chambers Street. Children in particular love the working models in the Hall of Power and the wildlife exhibits

NATIONAL LIBRARY OF SCOTLAND

George·IV Bridge
Widely used by historians and other researchers, the National Library of Scotland is the fourth largest in Britain and has the privilege of receiving a copy of every work published in Britain. Its 'parent' was the Advocates' Library, founded in 1682, for the benefit of Scotland's legal profession. In 1925 the Advocates' Library transferred all its non-legal works to the nation, thus forming the National Library.

NATIONAL MUSEUMS OF SCOTLAND

Royal Museum of Scotland, *Chambers Street* Formerly the Royal Scottish Museum, it shows the influence of London's Crystal Palace in its elegant, soaring cast-iron columns and balconies. Within its airy, spacious interior, with many halls and galleries, is an extremely wide-ranging collection, including decorative arts of the world, archaeology, ethnography, natural history, geology, technology and science. There is also a programme of special exhibitions as well as gallery talks, lectures and films.

Royal Museum of Scotland, *Queen Street* Formerly the National Museum of Antiquities, this museum traces the story of Scotland from the Stone Age right up to modern times, by way of the earliest artefacts from prehistory, through the Picts, Romans and Vikings, and on to the Dark Ages and the Middle Ages. More recently-recorded history on display includes relics of Mary, Queen of Scots and Bonnie Prince Charlie.

Sharing the same fine red sandstone building (1889) as the Royal Museum of Scotland (Queen Street), the **National Portrait Gallery** serves to bring to life many famous historical figures—the nation's kings and queens, rebels, Highland chiefs, political and literary figures, from the days of Queen Margaret right down to the 20th century in a very wide-ranging collection. There is also an extensive reference facility with engravings and photographs of many portraits.

PALACE OF HOLYROODHOUSE

Legend tells that the Scottish King David I was out hunting in the then darkly forested slopes of Holyrood Park when he was attacked and unhorsed by a wounded stag. Suddenly, a crucifix appeared between its antlers, the king grasped it and the stag fled. (This legend occurs in European literature attached to other places and saints.) In thanksgiving, the king founded the Abbey of Holyrood in 1128 and it adopted the stag and cross on its seal, as did the later burgh of Canongate nearby, which sprang up as a result of the Abbey.

King Edward of England burned the Abbey in 1322, and this fate at the hands of English invaders befell it again in 1544 and 1547. Just after Mary, Queen of Scots' association with it, the

Scottish Reformers did as much damage by demolishing the choir and transepts, around 1569.

In the 17th century King James VII converted it to a Roman Catholic Chapel Royal. It was violated again by a Presbyterian faction shortly after. As late as 1758 a new stone roof was built—but this collapsed only 10 years later. Today, 12th- or early 13th-century features include the north wall of the roofless nave and the great west doorway. The traceried windows are 17th-century.

The Palace of Holyroodhouse, which overlaps the outlines of the old religious buildings, grew originally from the Abbey guest house. It, too, has had a stormy history, bound up with the story of Scotland's Stuart monarchy. Holyroodhouse was founded by King James IV at the end of the 15th century, subsequently extended by his son, James V, damaged, like the Abbey, by the Earl of Hertford's raids in 1544 and 1547 but repaired for Mary, Queen of Scots, who held court here between 1561–7.

After the Union of the Crowns with England in 1603, Holyrood no longer had a monarch in residence. In 1650, fire damaged the Palace while it was occupied by Cromwell's troops. Though Cromwell was

responsible for some reconstruction, Charles II in 1671 ordered the rebuilding and redesigning which resulted in the façade seen today. Even then, it still saw some drama—an anti-Catholic mob ran rampage in it in 1688 and Prince Charles Edward Stuart held court here in 1745—even though the Castle, at the other end of the Royal Mile, held out against him.

Though George IV stayed in 1822, the royal residence was then in decline, with the emphasis on other parts of the growing city. However, Queen Victoria and later King George V renewed interest, with subsequent redecoration and revitalisation of the historic building.

Mary, Queen of Scots is very closely associated with Holyrood. After her return from France in 1561, this striking young widow turned the Palace into a glittering residence where balls and banquets were held—much to the disapproval of John Knox, who met with her several times in Holyrood. She married her second husband, Darnley, there in 1564. Later, the Palace gained its sinister associations as the scene of the murder of David Rizzio, the Queen's secretary, whom her husband and a band of jealous and ambitious conspirators thought was gaining too much of Mary's attention.

After the mystery of Darnley's death at the Kirk o' Field, her third marriage, to Bothwell, was conducted, according to Protestant rites this time, in the Palace's great hall, demolished in the rebuilding in Charles II's time in the 17th century. Mary left Holyrood for the last time after the confrontation with her opponents, the Lords of the Congregation, on Carberry Hill. After her surrender, she briefly returned to the Palace before being led away to captivity in Loch Leven Castle in 1567.

Except when the Royal Family is in residence, most of Holyrood is today open to view. The oldest part seen by the visitor is the James V Tower, the northernmost (or left hand) tower on the frontage—and the only surviving 16th-century part. It contains Mary's rooms on the second floor. This is the suite associated with the murder of Rizzio and a plaque marks the fatal spot. The Audience Chamber, where she argued with John Knox, retains its original panelled ceiling, while Mary's Bedroom has ceiling decoration which includes the monograms of her parents. Period furniture contributes to the atmosphere. On the floor below are Darnley's Rooms, altered in the 17th-century remodelling and featuring fine panelling, fireplaces, plasterwork and tapestries.

Along the frontage adjoining the James V Tower with the later Charles II Tower are the Duchess of Hamilton's Room and the Adam-style Royal Dining Room. Adjacent to it is the Grand Stair with its decoration of broadswords by Ferrara, the Italian craftsman. Down the southern side of the range, visitors will find the Throne Room and the Evening and Morning Drawing Rooms, chiefly used for ceremonial or social occasions. Most of the furniture is 18th-century. At the back of the Palace visitors can see three further rooms, also with fine furniture, tapestries and panelling, including the King's Bedchamber with its restored State Bed! Another major feature is the Picture Gallery with its collection of portraits of Scottish monarchs. They start with Fergus I in 330BC and, more than 80 portraits later, end with King James VII. Naturally, many are invented likenesses—and some are even invented monarchs—as the work was carried out by a single painter, a Dutchman, Jacob de Wet in 1684–5. This gallery was the scene of Bonnie Prince Charlie's levées during his brief occupation.

The setting for today's garden parties is in the gardens around the Palace; here also the ceremonial guards, the Royal Company of Archers, practise. A curiosity outside the Palace proper is the so-called Queen Mary's Bath House. This is a two-storey building with rubble walls dating from the 16th-century, probably built as a pavilion for tennis players.

Full of historic details inside and out, the Palace of Holyroodhouse offers an insight into the turbulence of Scottish history from the early Stewart Kings to the present day.

The royal palace at the foot of the Royal Mile, has for over nine centuries been the scene of pomp and ceremony – and of murder and intrigue. Inset: the Morning Drawing Room with its splendid fireplace of black veined marble, and elaborate plaster ceiling.

PARLIAMENT HOUSE

High Street
Tucked inconspicuously behind the High Kirk of St Giles are the buildings associated with Scotland's own independent parliament, which last sat in 1707. The early parliaments sat in Edinburgh Castle or the Tolbooth, but Charles I proposed the building of a Parliament House in 1632. Though later extensively altered for the needs of the legal profession, the Parliament Hall still has its original hammerbeam roof; the Laigh Hall also has some original features. Its neo-classical façade, obvious from Parliament Square, is by Robert Reid.

One-time Portobello resident—Sir Harry Lauder

PORTOBELLO

A sailor, George Hamilton, who had seen action during the capture of the town of Puerto Bello, on the isthmus of Panama in 1739, is credited with naming Edinburgh's seaside resort. He built the first house amongst the broom and rough grasses of the empty lands between the city and Musselburgh. Then beds of clay were discovered, which rapidly led to the development of brickworks and potteries. Soon, industry and resort developments proceeded in parallel.

Though the potteries have gone, the small-scale Georgian and later Victorian resort architecture survives—as does the promenade of 1860. Bracing walks, sea air and fairground fun are still on offer at the capital's own resort.

PRINCES STREET & THE GARDENS

Though for long the main shopping area in Edinburgh, Princes Street was originally intended as an elegant residential street. Its unique open atmosphere owes its existence to its early residents fighting long legal battles to ensure their views remained unspoiled by commercial developments. They secured this right by an Act of 1827. Even by this time, Princes Street was becoming a shopping concourse, though Princes Street Gardens remained private—the western gardens were laid out by 1820 and the eastern part by 1830 for the exclusive use of the residents, just as the Queen Street Gardens remain today.

However, by 1850, moves were made to make the gardens open to all—they were in any case being altered with the arrival of the railway. Today, visitors can stroll in pleasure-grounds which were once under the waters of the Nor' Loch, part of the city's defences made in 1460 by damming a stream where the North Bridge now stands. David Livingstone, explorer, Adam Black, former Lord Provost, and Allan Ramsay, poet, are some of the eminent Scots whose statues can be seen on a stroll in the gardens. The Scottish American War Memorial is also to be found there, and the popular attraction of the floral clock, just west of the Mound.

Jenners, Princes Street, inside and out— Edinburgh's answer to Harrods

REGISTER HOUSE

Princes Street
Considered to be a public building of the very highest architectural quality, this 'custom-built' record office by Robert Adam was started in 1774. Money from estates of Jacobite landowners forfeited after the Battle of Culloden went towards its construction. It was not finally completed till 1827 and now contains many famous documents of Scotland's history including the Scottish copy of the 1707 Treaty of Union with England. Its search rooms are open to the public.

ROYAL BOTANIC GARDENS

Inverleith

A plaque in today's Waverley Station marks the site of an early 'Physic Garden', which was started at Holyrood, 1670. About a century later, it was moved to a site on Leith Walk, then finally to its present site at Inverleith in 1823. Now, more than half a million visitors annually enjoy the forward planning of earlier generations of botanists. While academic research goes on in the background, everyday visitors enjoy the 70 acres of seclusion only minutes from the city centre—and perhaps learn from the informal demonstration garden and exhibition hall.

Other aspects of this fine botanical assembly include the largest collection of rhododendrons in Britain, an arboretum, peat garden, woodland garden, rock and heath gardens, a magnificent herbaceous border and extensive indoor collections—from cacti and succulents, ferns and orchids, to temperate species. The low hill on which Inverleith House is built in the centre of the garden offers fine views over the greenery to the city-centre skyline.

ROYAL COMMONWEALTH POOL

Only a few moments from Holyrood Park, the Royal Commonwealth Pool is a very popular facility, originally built for the Commonwealth Games in 1970. It is the city's largest swimming pool, Olympic standard, and also offers smaller pools, sauna and a fitness centre.

ROYAL HIGH SCHOOL

Regent Road

A school which traces its history at least to 1519, the Royal High School opened on its Calton Hill site in 1829. The building, with its outstanding neo-classical façade, was designed by Thomas Hamilton and complements the architecture of the other monuments higher up the hill. There is a good view of the school and beyond from Salisbury Crags in Holyrood Park.

The Royal High School vacated the building in 1969 and since that date conversion work has taken place to prepare it for possible political use as the venue for a Scottish Assembly.

ROYAL OBSERVATORY

Blackford Hill

At the Royal Observatory Visitor Centre is the largest telescope in Scotland and a range of exhibits on the theme of astronomy—as well as a fine view of Edinburgh and an astronomy bookshop. The Observatory started life on Calton Hill but was moved to a site where the air was clearer in 1895. Blackford Hill, where it now stands, is a park owned by the city since 1884 and offers fine walks by its pond and into the sheltering, tall trees of Blackford Dell.

ST GILES

High Street

Once the only parish church within the Old Town walls, the High Kirk of St Giles has been greatly altered over the centuries. In 1633 it briefly acquired cathedral status. It was the

The eagle, sign of the Evangelist, in St Giles

setting of a famous local incident in 1637 when a town resident, Jenny Geddes, threw a stool at the preacher, who was attempting to read a newly introduced English liturgy.

Parts of the pillars below the crown spire are 12th-century, the choir dates from 1460 and the distinctive spire from 1500. The building was refaced in a smooth stone during a controversial restoration by William Burn in 1829; only the spire escaped this treatment. The most recent part is the Chapel of the Most Ancient and Most Noble Order of the Thistle, designed by Sir Robert Lorimer in 1910. Immediately behind St Giles, to the south, is Parliament Square, built over the kirkyard in which John Knox was buried.

The pond at the Royal Botanic Gardens

SCOTT MONUMENT

Princes Street Gardens
This unmistakable, ornately Gothic spire dominates the east end of Princes Street and is also easily visible from South St David Street on the west side of St Andrew Square. A monument to one of Scotland's most enduring writers, Sir Walter Scott, it is 200ft (61m) high and was built 1840–6. It was created by George Meikle Kemp, a country joiner and self-taught architect who won the open architectural competition to design a suitable memorial. (Unfortunately Kemp died by drowning in the Union Canal while his work was under construction.)

A marble statue of Scott with his dog, by Thomas Steell, sits in the centre of the monument. Today's visitors can enjoy spectacular views after climbing the 287 steps to the top.

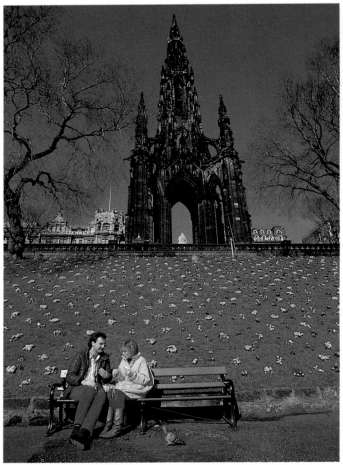

A marble statue of Sir Walter Scott sits beneath the Gothic fantasy that is the Scott Monument

Children will enjoy sitting on some of the tractors that their forefathers used, when they visit the Scottish Agricultural Museum

SCOTTISH AGRICULTURAL MUSEUM

Ingliston
The varied farming methods of the nation's agricultural heritage—tools, equipment, photographs, plus models and displays—provide an insight into life on the land. In addition to extensive displays, fully-furnished room settings give a glimpse into the former living conditions of farmers and crofters in the Lowlands and Highlands. Only a part of this wide-ranging collection is on display at any one time.

SCOTTISH NATIONAL GALLERY OF MODERN ART

Belford Road
From its previous home in Inverleith House, in the centre of the city's Botanic Gardens, this collection was moved to the classical setting of the former John Watson's School (1823). Here the visitor can see examples of all the main forms of 20th-century art by many famous artists and sculptors, such as Hockney, Hepworth, Picasso, and Moore. There is a changing programme of exhibitions.

SWANSTON

Tucked between the long slopes of the Pentlands and the encroaching suburban edges of the city and its bypass, Swanston still retains the charm and seclusion that Robert Louis Stevenson knew. The Stevensons had a summer cottage here during the 1870s and the area is mentioned in his *St Ives*; the author gleaned much material from a local shepherd. This tiny unspoilt 18th-century community is a conservation area and offers walks into the Pentland Hills beyond.

TRON CHURCH

High Street
The spire of the Tron Church is a conspicuous landmark on Edinburgh's skyline, though the church itself has not been used as a place of worship since 1952. Built by 1647, its original steeple was burned down in Edinburgh's own Great Fire in 1824. The building of both North and South Bridges in the 1780s had already altered the shape of the church, as the transepts were removed or shortened to allow the bridges' construction. Now owned by the town, the church's future seems likely to involve some kind of visitor facility.

UNIVERSITY OF EDINBURGH

Perhaps the most impressive of the many scattered uiversity buildings is the Old College on South Bridge, originally designed by Robert Adam in 1789. It was not finished until 1834 since the Napoleonic Wars intervened, and then to a modified design by William Playfair. Other notable buildings include the Italianate McEwan Hall (1897) in Teviot Place and, nearby, the Venetian-style Medical School (1888).

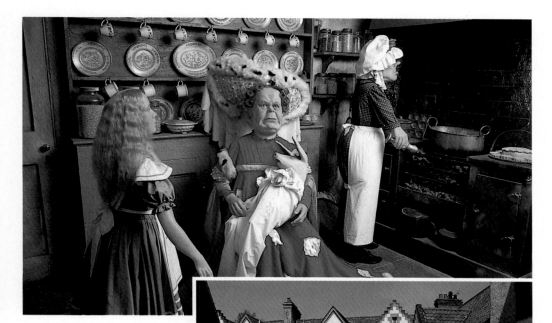

Alice, in a waxworks wonderland.
Right: White Horse Close

Further university developments can be seen in the George Square area. This was originally the first residential development outside the Old Town, completed speculatively by around 1766. Sir Walter Scott's parents lived at No. 25. However, only the west side and a small portion of the east side remains of the original work.

USHER HALL

Lothian Road
Edinburgh's premier concert hall was built in 1913 with a gift of £10,000 given in 1896 by Sir John Usher, of a prominent distilling family. A grand baroque-style octagon with a copper dome, it is easily recognised by the visitor.

WATER OF LEITH

While hardly on the same scale as the substantial rivers flowing through other Scottish towns, like the Clyde, the Tay or the Dee, nevertheless the little Water of Leith in its time helped promote many industries in Edinburgh. Rising in the Pentland Hills and entering the sea at Leith, the waters once powered corn and paper mills at Balerno, snuff mills at Currie and Juniper Green and other commercial activities. Several stretches of the river offer a 'green lung' to the city by means of walkways—pleasantly landscaped paths.

WAX MUSEUM

High Street
Down one of the High Street's many closes, New Assembly Close, the Edinburgh Wax Museum is housed in the 1766 New Assemblies Hall, which has had a varied history. Once it hosted dancing classes, at one stage it was a Masonic Lodge which Sir Walter Scott attended, later it was used by the Commercial Bank, till 1847. Now, it contains a display of figures from Scotland's past and present, some real, some fictional—even its Chamber of Horrors has a Scottish flavour. It includes Burke and Hare, the infamous local body-snatchers.

WEST REGISTER HOUSE

Charlotte Square
Designed by Robert Reid and originally opened in 1814 as St George's Church, the Town Council of the day intended the church to serve the inhabitants of the rapidly extending New Town. By the 1960s, the problems of a dwindling congregation and extensive refurbishment were solved by its conversion into an extension of the nation's main record office at Register House. It became West Register House and thus the spectacular copper dome, seen from all parts of George Street, was preserved. Exhibitions in the entrance hall show some of Scotland's important historical documents.

WHITE HORSE CLOSE

Canongate
This is a picturesque restoration, off the Canongate, of a former coaching inn and its courtyard, dating from the 17th century. The 'white horse' is said to recall a favourite palfrey of Mary, Queen of Scots. The White Horse Inn was the starting point of an early stagecoach service to London. It was also the quarters of Bonnie Prince Charlie's officers when he occupied the city during the final Jacobite rebellion in 1745. The inn and adjoining buidings are now residential property.

CITY WALKS

*This stunning fountain in Festival Square is a recent
addition to the City centre*

The Bridges and Calton Hill

*E*dinburgh has several bridges which you may well cross without realising that you are actually on a bridge at all. Within a close radius of the city centre you can cross George IV Bridge, South Bridge, North Bridge and Regent Bridge. Then you are at Calton Hill which offers the best view of Edinburgh.

Allow ¾ hour

The sturdy 18th-century North Bridge as seen from atop the Waverley Market, Princes Street

Begin at the corner of George IV Bridge and the High Street

1 GEORGE IV BRIDGE
This bridge was designed by Thomas Hamilton and completed in 1836. Named after the king who made a historic visit in 1822, this bridge provided Edinburgh with a southern approach to the city under the 1827 Improvement Act. On this walk the first road the bridge crosses over is called the Cowgate and the second is Merchant Street.

Proceed forward and the first building on your left is the National Library of Scotland.

2 THE NATIONAL LIBRARY OF SCOTLAND
Designed in 1934–6 by Reginald Failie. The steel frame was built in 1939 and the building was completed in 1950–5. There is the royal coat of arms over the front door and the tall figures on the front wall are the work of the sculptor Hew Lorimer. This library was orginally founded in 1682. Today the library has nearly 4,500,000 books and an extensive collection of

The National Library of Scotland holds a copy of every UK publication

manuscripts. It is one of the four largest libraries in Great Britain.

Directly across the road is Edinburgh Central Library.

3 EDINBURGH CENTRAL LIBRARY
This library has an extensive collection of reference and lending books. The Edinburgh Room is a must for visitors and locals seeking information on the city, past and present. They hold original old newspapers, maps, prints, and periodicals as well as books. Funds for the building of this library were donated to the city by the famous philanthropist, Andrew Carnegie. Designed between 1887 and 1890, the base of the building stands in the Cowgate, four storeys below.

Carry on across the bridge and take in the view of the Cowgate over the side. Turn left on to Chambers Street and on the right is the Royal Museum of Scotland.

4 THE ROYAL MUSEUM OF SCOTLAND
The Royal Museum of Scotland is a national institution and is the largest comprehensive museum in Europe. The range and quality of the collections are so varied that there is something to appeal to visitors of all ages and interests. The collection is housed in one of the finest Victorian buildings in the country – the visitor is immediately impressed by the main hall, which is a magnificent example of Victorian architecture.

After the Royal Museum of Scotland, keep on the same side of the road and turn right on to West College Street and then left into South College Street. At the foot of this street turn left on to South Bridge. Walk a few yards and then turn left into Old College

5 OLD COLLEGE
The outside of the Quadrangle was designed in 1789 by Robert Adam, the famous Scottish architect, and is believed to be his greatest public work. The interior was designed by the architect William Playfair, and built between 1819 and 1827. The dome was added in 1879. The front

of the building is made from Craigleith stone. The Talbot Rice Art Centre is situated in the Old College building. It houses the Torrie Collection which is a permanent display of 16th- and 17th-century European painting and sculpture and is displayed in the great gallery designed by William Playfair.

Come back into South Bridge and head further down the hill. About 200yds further on enjoy the view from this bridge on to the Cowgate.

6 SOUTH BRIDGE
In 1785 an act was passed authorising the building of South Bridge. It was eventually completed in 1788. The South Bridge spans the Cowgate as does George IV Bridge. At the junction of South Bridge and the High Street is the Tron Kirk where on New Year's Eve thousands of locals meet to bring in the New Year. Today South Bridge is a very busy area of the city.

On reaching the junction of South Bridge and the High Street cross straight over on to North Bridge. Continue on and stop after you pass the Scotsman offices on the left-hand side.

7 THE NORTH BRIDGE
Beneath the bridge and stretching the full length of Princes Street to the left used to be the Old Nor' Loch, a lake which protected Edinburgh's Old Town from attack. With a city wall built around the other areas of the Old Town, Edinburgh was a well-protected capital city. The Nor' Loch took 61 years to be fully drained, from 1759 to 1820. Beneath the bridge today is Waverley Railway Station and the rest of the old loch is now Princes Street Gardens. The foundation stone for the first North Bridge was laid in October 1763 by Lord Provost Drummond. The Bridge was opened in 1769 but after only a few months a section collapsed killing five people. After several

Scottish Americans who died during the American Civil War. To the left of Abraham Lincoln there is a circular memorial to the Scottish philosopher, David Hume. The memorial was designed by Robert Adam. The large needle-like monument in the centre of the burial ground is in memory of several political martyrs and was erected in 1844.

Leave the cemetery and turn right heading further along Waterloo Place until the junction with Regent Road. Cross the road and go up the steps leading to Calton Hill.

10 CALTON HILL

This is where you have one of the finest all-round views of Edinburgh. As you walk up the steps to the top of the hill, the first monument on the left is to Dugald Stewart, a professor of moral philosophy at Edinburgh University. The 12 columns form the National Monument, intended to be a replica of the Parthenon in Athens; unfortunately the subscriptions ran out and it was never completed. Calton Hill used to house Edinburgh's observatory which has now moved to Blackford Hill. The Old Observatory which remains on Calton Hill was designed by the planner of Edinburgh's New Town, James Craig. The Nelson Monument, like an upturned telescope, was designed shortly after the Battle of Trafalgar by Robert Burn.

disputes about responsibility the bridge was re-opened in 1772. The present bridge dates back to 1897.

Continue to the foot of North Bridge and turn right past the Post Office until you reach Regent Bridge.

8 REGENT BRIDGE

This small bridge was designed by Archibald Elliot in 1815 and was built between 1816 and 1819. It is also a war memorial to the men who lost their lives during the Napoleonic War. The bridge carries Waterloo Place over Calton Road.

Continue along Waterloo Place until there is an entrance in to the right for Calton Cemetery.

9 CALTON CEMETERY

This burial ground contains several interesting monuments including a statue of Abraham Lincoln, which was erected to the memory of the

The South Bridge spans the Canongate

Greyfriars Kirkyard

Greyfriars Kirkyard has more famous people buried in it than anywhere else in Scotland. There are 56 famous Scots buried in marked graves and several others buried in unmarked graves somewhere in the Kirkyard. There is a simple route around the graves to see the headstones of some of the more famous names.

Allow about 1 hour

Begin at the entrance of Greyfriars Kirk, which is at the junction of George IV Bridge and Candlemaker Row. The first gravestone is to the famous Skye terrier dog, Greyfriars Bobby.

1   GREYFRIARS BOBBY

Bobby was a Skye terrier who was owned by a man called John Gray, known in the town as Old Jock. After Jock died in 1858 the dog went to his graveside every day for 14 years, only leaving to get his lunch at the local tavern each day on hearing the one o'clock gun. The Lord Provost of the day presented Bobby with an inscribed collar, which, along with his dish and other items, are to be found in Huntly House Museum. Greyfriars Bobby eventually died on 14 January 1872, at the age of 16. This stone was erected by the Dog Aid Society and unveiled in 1981 by HRH The Duke of Gloucester. A bronze statue, by William Brodie, was erected near the churchyard in memory of the faithful animal.

Directly ahead of this gravestone is Greyfriars Kirk.

2   GREYFRIARS KIRK

The church is built on a site of a Franciscan friary (1447–1560) and was dedicated on Christmas Day 1620. It was here the National Covenant was first signed – a protest against the religious policy of Charles I. Gaelic services are still held here on Sundays at 4pm. The church was heavily restored in 1938 by Henry Kerr.

Turn right and follow the path down the hill, parallel with Candlemaker Row, until a block of red granite stone on the left marks the front of John Gray's grave.

3   JOHN GRAY

John Gray, a local police constable, was the master of Greyfriars Bobby. He died in 1858 and was buried in a grave covered by red granite stone. The gravestone was erected by the American lovers of Bobby. Because of the dog's devotion to his master the Lord Provost presented him with a collar which signified that he was exempt from the 1867 law which required all dogs in Edinburgh to be licensed.

Continue down the hill. The last monument on the right-hand side is the Martyrs' Monument.

4   THE MARTYRS' MONUMENT

From 27 May 1661 and the execution of the Marquis of Argyll by beheading to 17 February 1688 when James Renwick was executed, 18,000 martyrs were executed in Edinburgh. Thousands of people gathered at public executions, and it is said that the roll of the execution drums was drowned out by the singing of psalms.

Turn to face away from this monument, continue forward and turn right onto the path to proceed down the hill. Follow the path which bears left and the first flat grave on the left is that of the New Town architect, James Craig.

5   JAMES CRAIG

James Craig designed the first stage of Edinburgh's New Town. He won the competition to design a new town for Edinburgh on 17 April 1767. For his plan 23-year-old Craig was presented with a gold medal with the Freedom of the City in a silver box. His design was simple but very effective, it comprised a gridiron of broad streets with a spacious square at each end of the main street. His plan showed uniformity in the size and appearance of the houses. Sadly, he died a poor man, virtually a forgotten figure.

The next important grave is more like a small tree stump. It is situated on the grass and is marked with the initials JEM. It is the grave of James, Earl of Morton.

6   THE REGENT MORTON

James Douglas, 4th Earl of Morton (1516–81) succeeded the Earl of Mar as Regent during the childhood of James VI, the Son of Mary, Queen of Scots. He held the position of Regent for six years and was influential in the building of the Half Moon Battery at Edinburgh Castle which still survives today. Morton was involved in the murder of Mary, Queen of Scots' secretary, David Rizzio, and was convicted and executed as an accessory to the murder of Mary's husband Henry, Lord Darnley.

The path now ends so you must cut over the grass to the left and head towards the stone steps. There are 10 steps in total. After the steps behind the second tree is the grave of John Porteous.

7   JOHN PORTEOUS

He was head of Edinburgh's City Guard, the organisation which preceded the present police force. In 1736, at the execution of a smuggler called Andrew Wilson, it is said that John Porteous gave the order to his men to fire shots into the rowdy crowd. Some were killed and others injured. He was tried and sentenced to be hanged for his actions. The Edinburgh mob decided they could not wait for justice to be carried out, so they broke into the Tolbooth Prison, dragged Porteous to the Grassmarket and carried out the execution themselves. This event is now known as the Porteous Riots.

Continue forward. At the end of the path is the grave of Walter Scott.

8 WALTER SCOTT

Here lies the father of Sir Walter Scott, the famous Scottish writer and author of *Ivanhoe* and the *Waverley* novels. Walter Scott was a solicitor and writer to the Signet. His wife was Anne Rutherford and they produced 13 children, the youngest son becoming Sir Walter Scott. Unfortunately, the first children died in infancy. Walter lived in College Wynd and that was where Sir Walter was born. They were all, however, soon to move to 25 George Square.

Turn right and walk towards the gates of George Heriot's School.

9 GEORGE HERIOT'S SCHOOL

George Heriot was appointed goldsmith to the king in 1601 and was known in the town by the name 'Jinglin' Geordie'. After his death in 1623 he left his fortune to the Edinburgh Town Council for the education of fatherless boys. The construction of Heriot's Hospital was started in 1628. Cromwell used it as a military hospital in 1650 but the building was not completed until 1659. In that year it accepted 30 fatherless boys. This is one of the finest buildings erected in 17th-century Scotland and still houses George Heriot's School.

Facing away from the school gates, take the first lane on the left, which leads to the grave of William Creech. His headstone is the seventh on the right.

10 WILLIAM CREECH

This man was Robert Burns' Edinburgh publisher and he also published the works of the Scottish economist, Adam Smith. He was Lord Provost of Edinburgh from 1811 to 1813. Creech became very rich by buying copyrights, initially for an extremely small sum. Earlier in 1788 he had been on the jury at the trial of Deacon Brodie. Brodie was a well-respected citizen by day, but by night he was a rogue, robber and gambler. Robert Louis Stevenson was later to base his story *Dr Jekyll and Mr Hyde* on Deacon Brodie.

Walk back towards the school. Turn left and leave the West Yard. Bear right and then follow the path by turning right. The last monument on the right is the large Adam Mausoleum.

11 THE ADAM MAUSOLEUM

Here is buried William Adam, the celebrated architect and father of two even more successful sons. His son, Robert, is perhaps the best known architect in the family. He designed Charlotte Square, Register House and the Old Quad at Edinburgh University. William himself was involved in the design of the first Royal Infirmary and the

Many Edinburgh notables rest in peace in Greyfriars Churchyard

New Exchange, which is now the City Chambers of Edinburgh.

Turn left and walk along by the back wall of the Kirkyard. The large rounded mausoleum on the right is to Sir George Mackenzie.

12 SIR GEORGE MACKENZIE

The prosecution of Covenanters and others accused of plotting against the king was conducted by the Lord Advocate, Sir George Mackenzie. He boasted in 1680 that he had never lost a case for the king and was known to the Covenanters as 'Bluidy Mackenzie'. In 1689 he established the Advocates' Library which is now the National Library of Scotland. In 1783 an 18-year-old boy spent six weeks in this mausoleum after escaping from the old Tolbooth Prison.

Follow the path round to the gates, the way out of Greyfriars Kirkyard.

George Heriot's—a much-respected school for over 300 years

Cramond Village

Cramond is a peaceful 18th-century village on the outskirts of Edinburgh. The houses are huddled round the mouth of the River Almond. Cramond's harbour has a great history, stretching back through the centuries to Roman times.

EDINBURGH

Cramond Island

Granton

Leith

Cranlond

B9085

A90

New Town

A902

Murrayfield

A8

Arthur's Seat

A1

A71

A702

A68

The map above is for location purposes only. Cramond lies approximately six miles from the centre of Edinburgh and there are regular bus services from Princes Street (check locally for bus numbers and times). Drivers will take the A90 (Queensferry Road) from the west end of Princes Street and proceed to Cramond Road South.

Allow 1 hour

Start at the point of the small headland at the mouth of the river.

The River Almond tumbles in a noisy torrent down the weir at Cramond

1   CRAMOND ISLAND

Not far from the shore lies Cramond Island, a favourite place of Robert Louis Stevenson, author of *Treasure Island.* The island was inhabited until 1947 and can still be visited today at low tide. (Be careful not to get caught by the tide.) Across the Firth of Forth are the shores of Fife. Sometimes oil rigs can be seen on the horizon, waiting to be towed out to the North Sea oilfields. The Drum sands are teeming with sea birds and the waters round here were once famous for their oysters.

Turn left and walk upriver until you are opposite the harbour-mouth buildings.

2   CRAMOND HARBOUR

This peaceful harbour was once a bustling workplace. It was first used by the Romans for bringing in supplies by sea to their fort. It was later a fishing port and then an important centre for the import and export of iron goods. The buildings here have been well restored. Originally many would have been simple 'biggings' with turf roofs and earth floors.

Proceed a short distance upriver to the steps on the right-hand side.

3   CRAMOND FERRY

Surely one of the shortest (and cheapest) ferry trips in Scotland. It is a voyage of about two minutes from the Cramond side of the river to the opposite bank. The ferry provides access to Dalmeny Woods and grounds, property of the Earl of Rosebery. This is a popular area for walks and picnics, particularly pretty in springtime. It is possible to continue through the Rosebery estate to South Queensferry. There is a small charge for the crossing and the ferry times are:
Summer
April – September
9am – 7pm
Winter
October – March
10am – 4pm
Continue upriver to the boatsheds on the left-hand side.

4   CRAMOND BOAT CLUB

Meet *Lucinda, Mairi Ruth* or *Graculus,* vessels of the Cramond Boat Club which was founded in 1934. In the winter they lie like stranded seals on the quayside; in early April a crane arrives to release them again in the river.

Follow the river to the ruined mill buildings at the weir.

5   FAIR-A-FAR MILL

The mill dam and ruin of a forge remain beside the river. They provide a reminder of the days when there used to be five independent mills in this area. Marks on the south-west wall of the building show the position of the old mill wheel. Between 1752 and 1860 nails, shovels, hoops, chains, anchors and other iron products were manufactured here. A skilled nail maker could produce about 1,200 nails a day, earning about one shilling per week. Iron came in to Cramond from Russia and Sweden and, once transformed, the products went as far afield as Spain and the West Indies. By 1810 Cramond was no longer an important iron works, but one of the mills did continue in paper production till 1881.

Return downstream turning right, up the hill, just past Caddell's cottages.

6 SCHOOL BRAE

At the top of School Brae, the building on the right, appropriately enough, is the Infant Department of Cramond School. On the left is the village Post Office.

At the top of School Brae turn left, and continue to Cramond Glebe Road. Turn left and go downhill to the old school house on the left.

7 THE OLD SCHOOL HOUSE

This building, now a private house, was used as a school till 1875. In 1764 it would have been ringing with the voices of 70 to 80 children who were under the guidance of the schoolmaster, Ninian Paton. This remarkable man took his post on 16 September 1764 and held his position for 52 years despite the fact that he was a heavy smoker. He had a very unusual crop growing in the schoolhouse garden as well – tobacco!

A short distance further on, turn left into the churchyard.

8 CRAMOND KIRK

There has been a church on this site for centuries. In 1656 it was described as being in a state of 'ruinousnes'. It was repaired and the present castellated parapet was added in 1811. The present incumbent is unlikely to have the same problem as the minister in 1691 who recorded that the service was disturbed by 'ye fighting of doges in ye Church'. Locals were instructed to keep their dogs at home in future.

Turn right and walk along the edge of the graveyard to the gate in the north east wall.

9 THE GRAVEYARD

Some of the graves are almost 300 years old. Look for those with the wonderful carvings of skulls, bones and hour-glasses, all signifying death. In complete contrast are the monuments to the Cadell family, who took over the iron mills down by the river in 1771. Appropriately, they were commemorated after death not in stone but in iron.

Leave the graveyard and walk towards the house directly opposite.

10 CRAMOND HOUSE

This is an H-plan house which dates from 1680. In its heyday it was visited by royalty. Queen Victoria visited the Duchess of Kent here before continuing her journey to her Highland home, Balmoral. The property is now owned by the Cramond Parish Church and is used as the beadle's residence.

Turn northwards towards Cramond Tower.

11 CRAMOND TOWER

This is a tall medieval defensive tower, date uncertain. One theory states that it was part of a palace belonging to the Bishop of Dunkeld. It fell into a ruinous state and the then Edinburgh Corporation began restoration work. This was suddenly halted when they realised that they didn't actually own it. It is now privately owned.

Follow the path round to the sign for the Roman camp on the left-hand side.

Cramond Kirkyard is entered via an elegant pair of iron gates

12 ROMAN FORT

Started about AD142 at the instruction of Emperor Antoninus Pius this was designed to protect the eastern flank of a defensive wall which stretched across Scotland (Antonine's Wall). There is a plan showing what the fort may have looked like next to the church. It covered a full six acres and at one time was manned by more than 900 men. The walls were stone-faced barriers of clay and turf, 27ft (8m) thick. Inside the fort were granaries, garrisons, workshops, latrines and a bath-house. Eventually these forces were pulled back behind the more famous Hadrian's Wall to the south.

The Celts called this place 'Caer Almond', 'fort on the Almond', hence the name by which it is still known.

The Romans recognised Cramond's strategic advantages and built a substantial fort here

The Water of Leith

*E*very great city has its river and Edinburgh is no exception. The Water of Leith may be much smaller than the Thames or the Seine, but in its heyday it was no less important to its city. This walk follows the river on parts of its journey through the heart of Edinburgh.

Allow ¾ hour

Begin in front of the Granary Bar in the Dragonara Hotel.

1 BELL'S MILL

The Water of Leith is approximately 22 miles (35km) long and along the river there are traces of at least 80 mills. Most of Bell's Mill was destroyed by an explosion in 1975.

The granary of Bell's Mill—now part of a hotel

The remaining granary is now part of the hotel. It was the last mill on the river to be worked commercially by water. One of its products, wood flour, was used in synthetic flooring, plastics and even explosives. High above the doorway a sheaf of corn and the date 1805 recall its day as a corn mill.

Walk downhill to the river which is behind the mill.

2 THE WATER OF LEITH

The characteristic brown tinge to the water comes from the peaty moorlands where it originates. The water quality is good and the river supports a population of trout throughout its course. In 1617 Leith water entered the law books. An Act of Scots Parliament stated that the Standard Pint Jug should contain, 'Three pounds seven ounces troy of clear running water of the Water of Leith'.

Walk downstream to the bridge.

3 BELFORD BRIDGE

This bridge was constructed between 1885 and 1887. The new walkway goes right underneath it. On the left-hand pier of the bridge it is possible to make out the City of Edinburgh's coat of arms. On the opposite side of the same pier is the Scottish royal coat of arms. The faintly visible motto is, *Nemo me impune lacessit*, 'No one shall attack me with impunity'.

Follow the path through the trees as far as the steps going up the river bank.

4 SUNBURY

The new houses along the opposite river bank are part of the Sunbury development. They take their name from the Sunbury Distillery which stood in this area. Also nearby was a tannery called the Leggate Skinworks. The large sheds on the opposite bank store wood for the Whytock and Reid Company whose cabinet factory was built by the river in 1886.

Climb the steps, turn right and proceed downhill to the centre of the old Dean Bridge.

5 DEAN VILLAGE

The word 'dene' or 'dean' means deep valley, but originally this picturesque area was known as the 'Village of the Water of Leith'. It grew up around the mills that had been here since the 12th century. At one time it was the centre of a community of Baxters (bakers) who operated 11 watermills along the river and two granaries in the area. Upstream on the right-hand side is the old school, now converted into flats. Opposite it, downstream, is the massive West Mill. Rebuilt in 1805, it is the largest surviving industrial building of its era. In the distance the Holy Trinity Church can be seen rising above the trees. It is no longer used but is preserved as an electricity sub-station.

Cross the bridge to the doorway opposite at the bottom of Bell's Brae.

6 BAXTERS' TOLBOOTH
This 17th-century building was the headquarters and granary of the Incorporation of Baxters (bakers). The carving over the doorway shows two baker's peels (shovels). On the peels are three cakes and a pie. The inscriptions read, 'God's providence is our inheritance' and 'God Bless the Baxters of Edinburgh who built this house in 1675'. The steep hill or 'brae' was once a main road out of Edinburgh. James Boswell and Dr Johnson clattered down it on their journey to the Hebrides.

From the Tolbooth turn left down Miller Row to the three mill stones set in the roadway.

7 LINDSAY'S MILL
This mill was situated virtually on top of the damhead which can still be glimpsed through the railings. Listening to the water roar, it is strange to think that in 1978 the Water of Leith was disappearing. Between Belford and Dean Bridges gallons of water were vanishing through the river bed. The cause is still a mystery.

Follow the path until you are opposite the Oxylitre building.

A shady glade beside the Water of Leith

8 MAR'S MILL
Mar's Mill originally stood on this site. The present neo-baronial building was erected by a publisher in 1912 as a racquets court. Today it is the home of Oxylitre, makers of anaesthetic and oxygen therapy equipment.

Walk underneath the bridge.

9 DEAN BRIDGE
Constructed in 1832 by the famous Scottish engineer, Thomas Telford, the bridge provided a new route out of Edinburgh and also access to new housing developments across the gorge. The bridge has been described as a 'dream in stone of a community and a brain belonging to a more gracious age'. It is 106ft (32m) high and cost £18,556 to build. The masonry piers are hollow and are regularly inspected. The raised parapet is the result of a report in 1886 on the 'Prevention of suicides at Dean Bridge'.

Take the path along the river to the circular Roman temple.

10 ST BERNARD'S WELL
In the 1800s the mineral waters here were very popular. The temple was originally built by a wealthy law lord who felt he had benefited from the waters. It was restored in 1888. The statue is of Hygeia, health personified. St Bernard's was not popular with everyone; a man called Forsyth in 1805 commented that 'this spring has a slight resemblance in flavour to the washings of a foul gun barrel'.

Continue to St Bernard's bridge.

11 ST BERNARD'S BRIDGE
A low bridge with Jacobean style steps added in 1887. This signifies almost the end of the Dean Gorge, an area where the Water of Leith acts as a boundary for six different units: parliamentary constituencies, municipal wards, postal districts and the Church of Scotland, Episcopal and Catholic parishes.

Go underneath the bridge, turn right and follow the river to the traffic lights.

12 STOCKBRIDGE
Another of the string of industrial villages along the river which at one time provided the city with foodstuffs, paper, leather, spices, snuff, glue, spirits, beer, rope, flax and wood, among other things. The road to the right leads up to the town centre. It leaves behind a river that has given much to the city and is still close to the hearts of many Edinburgh citizens – especially those of the Water of Leith Trust, founded in 1976. They are slowly transforming what Robert Louis Stevenson called 'that dirty Water of Leith' into something very beautiful.

Hygeia's temple at St Bernard's Well, designed by Alexander Naysmith

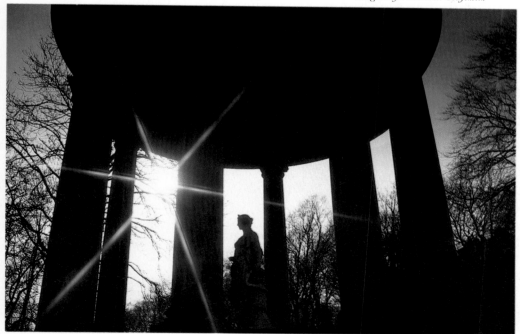

The New Town

*I*n 1767, James Craig a 23-year-old architect, won the competition to design a new town for Edinburgh. His simple but effective plan produced two fine squares and wide Georgian streets of extreme elegance. Today the New Town has some of the finest Georgian architecture in the whole of Europe.

Allow 1 hour

Start at the corner of South Charlotte Street and Charlotte Square at the house of Alexander Graham Bell.

1   ALEXANDER GRAHAM BELL

The inventor of the telephone was born here at 16 South Charlotte Street on 3 March 1847. He attended the Royal High School and then left for London and the USA. It was while he was Professor of Vocal Physiology at Boston University that he invented the telephone. He patented the idea in 1876.

Turn left into Charlotte Square. On the right, in the centre of the square, is a statue of Prince Albert on horseback.

2   PRINCE ALBERT

This statue was designed by John Steell and unveiled by Queen Victoria. She was so delighted with the statue that she called John Steell to Holyrood Palace and, on the same day, made him Sir John Steell. Queen Victoria and Prince Albert first visited Edinburgh in 1842. This visit was an embarrassment to the authorities as the Lord Provost, Sir James Forrest, overslept and failed to meet the Queen at the correct time.

Georgian elegance in the terraced north side of Charlotte Square, designed by Robert Adam

Continue forward. On the corner of Charlotte Square and Hope Street, above No 24, is the house where Douglas Haig was born.

3   DOUGLAS HAIG

The first Earl Haig was born in Edinburgh in 1861. In 1883 he went to Sandhurst and then travelled to India with the British army. He was a brigade major during the Boer War. After service in Egypt, South Africa and India he became Commander-in-Chief at the start of the First World War. It is believed that some of his orders committed the lives of many men when there was little chance of success. Also related to Haig are the founders of the famous whisky distilling firm, and Alexander Haig, former American Secretary of State.

Continue to walk round the square. The tall building on the left is West Register House.

4   WEST REGISTER HOUSE

This was formerly St George's Church, designed by Robert Reid and founded in 1811. It has been converted into a modern record repository which opened in 1971. It contains modern government records including the Scottish Railway archives, business archives, maps and plans. The Scottish Record Office Museum in the front hall contains a permanent exhibition of historic Scottish documents.

Continue around the square to Nos 1– 11, a block of buildings designed by Robert Adam.

5   Nos 1–11 CHARLOTTE SQUARE

This square provides the visitor with some of the finest Georgian architecture in the whole of Europe. No 1 has one of the best Georgian interiors in Edinburgh. No 5 is the headquarters of the National Trust for Scotland and No 6 is the official residence of the Secretary of State for Scotland. Meanwhile No 7 is the Georgian House, a superb Georgian-style house which is open to the public and is run by the National Trust. Between No 8 and No 9 there is a plaque on the wall recording that Lord Lister stayed here from 1870 to 1877. He was the pioneer of the carbolic spray as an antiseptic.

Leave Charlotte Square by George Street. Walk along George Street and turn left into North Castle Street. On the right at No 39 is the house which used to belong to Sir Walter Scott.

6   SIR WALTER SCOTT

He stayed at No 39 Castle Street periodically from 1802 to 1826. Born at the top of College Wynd, during his childhood he contracted polio. He was educated at the Royal High School and Edinburgh University. His first important literary work was *The Minstrelsy of the Scottish Border*. His later works include *Ivanhoe*, *Rob Roy* and the *Waverley* novels and the famous poem *The Lady of the Lake*. Sir Walter was created a Baronet in 1820 by George IV.

Carry on down the hill and turn right on to Queen Street. At No 51, on the right-hand side, there is the old house of Sir James Young Simpson.

Impressive bank headquarters dominate one side of St Andrew Square

7 SIR JAMES YOUNG SIMPSON

He stayed here in Queen Street for some time. It was he who discovered the anaesthetic properties of chloroform. Ether was discovered in America in 1846 and Simpson's discovery came in 1847. Chloroform became widely accepted after Queen Victoria used it during the birth of Prince Leopold. Having been made physician to the Queen of Scotland in 1847, Simpson was created a Baronet in 1866.

Continue along Queen Street and turn left into Frederick Street which is flanked on each side by Queen Street Gardens. Then turn right on to Heriot Row. At No 17 is the house of Robert Louis Stevenson.

8 ROBERT LOUIS STEVENSON

The author of well-known stories such as *Treasure Island, Kidnapped* and *The Strange Case of Dr Jekyll and Mr Hyde*. The Jekyll and Hyde tale may be based on a real Edinburgh character called Deacon Brodie who by day was a well-respected citizen but by night was a rogue, gambler and robber. In France, Stevenson married an American lady called Fanny Osbourne and was to travel to Tahiti, Hawaii and Samoa, where he died in 1894. *Treasure Island* is indeed a world-renowned story of high adventure.

Move along to Heriot Row and turn right on to Hanover Street. Walk to the top of this street and turn left on to George Street. After the George Hotel on the left there is St Andrew's and St George's Church.

9 ST ANDREW'S AND ST GEORGE'S CHURCH

This church was built to an oval design by Major Andrew Fraser and was opened for the first time in 1784. This was the first burgh church in the New Town and was named after Scotland's patron saint. The 168ft steeple was erected three years after the main building was built. The interior supports a superb Adam-style ceiling. One authority described the ceiling as 'one of the small masterpieces of 18th-century Edinburgh'.

Directly opposite the church is the fine building of the Royal Bank of Scotland.

10 THE ROYAL BANK OF SCOTLAND

In 1843 the directors of this bank purchased for £20,000 a building on this site which was the Royal College of Physicians and promptly razed it to the ground. The bank then built the present building on the site to the design of David Rhind. The foundation stone was laid on 4 June 1844 and the office opened for business in April 1847.

Continue along George Street and reach St Andrew Square. In the centre is the large monument to Henry Dundas, the 1st Viscount Melville.

11 THE MELVILLE MONUMENT

This monument was erected in 1823 in memory of Henry Dundas the 1st Viscount Melville (1742–1811). He was a dominant figure in politics and for over four decades he was treasurer to the Navy and Lord Advocate and Keeper to the Scottish Signet. The subscription for the monument was raised by members of the Royal Navy. It was designed by William Burn and the statue is by Chantrey.

Walk around the square and at its head, set back from the street, is another fine bank building, the Royal Bank of Scotland. Notice the out-of-proportion statue at the front of the building.

12 THE ROYAL BANK OF SCOTLAND

This building was at one time a splendid Georgian town house and was erected between 1772 and 1774 for Sir Lawrence Dundas. The site was originally intended for St Andrew's and St George's Church, which was relegated to nearby George Street.

Today it is the registered office of the Royal Bank of Scotland. Built of Ravelston stone, the house was designed by Sir William Chambers RA. Today's splendid banking hall was added in 1858 with its magnificent dome pierced by 120 stars. This section was designed by Peddie and Kinnear of Edinburgh who also designed the charmingly decorated staircase and probably the two-storeyed entrance hall. This fine building is where the walk ends.

Princes Street

The view of Edinburgh Castle from Princes Street is magnificent and Princes Street Gardens, which run parallel to the main street, are a joy to walk through. Princes Street is today the main shopping centre of Edinburgh.

Allow ¾ hour

Begin at the corner of North Bridge and Princes Street outside the main entrance to the North British Hotel.

1   THE NORTH BRITISH HOTEL
This hotel was designed by W Hamilton Beattie in a competition of 1895 and completed and opened on October 1902. The large clock tower is 190ft (58m) high and is one of Edinburgh's familiar landmarks. The clock is always 3 minutes fast so that people heading to the adjacent railway station will arrive in plenty of time for their train.
Opposite this hotel is Register House.

2   REGISTER HOUSE
This was the first important government building in the UK. Designed by Robert Adam, it is probably the finest classical building in Edinburgh. The foundation stone was laid on 27 June 1774. Register House stores Scotland's national records and it is often used by visitors tracing their Scottish ancestry. Outside the front of this building there is a bronze statue of the Duke of Wellington on his horse, Copenhagen. The statue was designed by Sir John Steell and is known as the Iron Duke in bronze by Steell.
Proceed along Princes Street. On the left, after the North British Hotel, is Waverley Market.

3   THE WAVERLEY MARKET
Directly above the Waverley Station, here is a good speciality shopping centre under one roof. There are many small, quality retailers specialising mainly in fashion and foods, including beauty products, jewellery, perfumes, knitwear and leather goods. The City of Edinburgh Tourist Information Centre is also situated here on street level. It provides a complete tourist and accommodation service for visitors to the capital.
Continue along the main street and cross Waverley Bridge on the left-hand side. Standing inside Princes Street Gardens there is a statue of David Livingstone.

4   DAVID LIVINGSTONE
David Livingstone was made an honorary Burgess of Edinburgh in 1857. Born in March 1813, he

Scott Monument amid the floral profusion of Princes St Gardens

became a missionary and was sent to Africa, where he crossed the Kalahari Desert, went up the Zambesi River and discovered the Victoria Falls. In 1865, Livingstone went in search of the sources of the Nile. He went missing for five years but was found safely by an American newspaper correspondent. When he died in May 1873, the nation mourned the loss.
Continue along Princes Street. The next tall monument on the left is the Scott Monument.

5   THE SCOTT MONUMENT
A monument to Sir Walter Scott, designed by George Meikle Kemp and built between 1840 and 1844. It takes the style of an elaborate Gothic spire and it is more than 200ft (61m) high. You can reach the top by walking up the 287 steps. The exterior of the monument is decorated with figures from Scottish history and characters from Scott's novels. In the centre is the marble statue of Sir Walter Scott with his dog, Maida, by his side.
Directly across the road is the famous department store, Jenners.

6   JENNERS DEPARTMENT STORE
This store is Edinburgh's equivalent of Harrods of London. The building was designed by William Hamilton Beattie in 1895 and is typical of a large Victorian store. When built this was one of the biggest department stores in Britain.
Proceed along Princes Street to the junction with the Mound where there are two large gallery buildings. On Princes Street is the Royal Scottish Academy and at the rear of this building is the National Gallery of Scotland.

Brash modern stores vie with sedate Victorian ones for the custom of Princes Street's shoppers

10 SIR JAMES YOUNG SIMPSON

This statue was designed by William Brodie in 1877. Sir James Young Simpson was born in Bathgate but he studied at Edinburgh University, starting his course at the age of 14. In 1847 he made the amazing discovery of the anaesthetic properties of chloroform. Simpson inspired such confidence in his discovery that Queen Victoria used chloroform at the birth of Prince Leopold in 1853. He became a Baronet in 1866.

Continuing towards the West End, reach St John's Episcopal Church on the left.

Centre-stage in Princes Street is given to the RSA with the National Gallery behind

7 THE ROYAL SCOTTISH ACADEMY/THE NATIONAL GALLERY

The RSA, on Princes Street, was designed by William Playfair and was completed in 1826. It was enlarged between 1833 and 1836. Above the portico entrance is a large statue of Queen Victoria, designed by John Steell. The National Gallery is also by William Playfair and is one of the more important of the smaller galleries of Europe. As well as paintings by Scotland's finest artists, works by masters such as Rubens, Turner and Gainsborough also hang here.

Cross the Mound and enter West Princes Street at the Floral Clock.

8 THE FLORAL CLOCK

This is the oldest Floral Clock in the world, built in 1903. A cuckoo pops out to mark every quarter hour. The flower arrangement each year is different and the layout will mark an important event to the city. Approximately 23,000 flowers are used in the clock, the circumference of which is 36ft (11m), the diameter 11ft (3m). The statue beside the clock is of the famous Scottish poet,

Alan Ramsay, writer of the religious satire *The Gentle Shepherd*. He opened in Edinburgh what is believed to be the oldest circulating library in Britain.

Walk through the Princes Street Gardens and pass a statue on the right-hand side, to the Royal Scots Greys and, on the left, the Ross Band Stand. Continue until, on the right-hand side, you reach a statue to Thomas Guthrie.

9 THOMAS GUTHRIE

Thomas Guthrie was a Church of Scotland minister who organised non-sectarian schools for poor children. He gained world-wide fame and his caring establishments became known as the 'Ragged Schools'. His knowledge of drunkenness among the poor led him to fight for control of the supply of liquor. He was one of the men responsible for the passing of the 1853 Act which cut back the hours of public houses and closed them completely on a Sunday.

Carry on straight ahead until you reach some steps which lead back on to the main street. On reaching the street you will see, directly on the right, a statue to Sir James Young Simpson.

11 ST JOHN'S EPISCOPAL CHURCH

This church is dated 1815–18 and was designed by William Burn. The cost of building it was £18,000, raised by Bishop Sandford from donations and an issue of shares. Burn's interior has been described as a masterpiece of its time. There is a convenient café in the basement of the church. The Scottish portrait painter, Raeburn, is buried in the mortuary chapel at the east end.

Turn left at the end of the church on to Lothian Road. You now see the large Caledonian Hotel.

12 THE CALEDONIAN HOTEL

This is one of the largest and most distinguished of Edinburgh's principal buildings. It opened for the first time in December 1903 and soon became one of the great railway hotels of Britain. Distinguished guests who have stayed here include Charles Chaplin, Laurel and Hardy, Ginger Rogers, Marlon Brando, Bob Hope and Bing Crosby. Even Roy Rogers and his 'wonder horse' Trigger stayed here in March 1954.

OUT OF CITY

T·O·W·N·A·N·D·C·I·T·Y·G·U·I·D·E·S

AA

T·O·W·N·A·N·D·C·I·T·Y·G·U·I·D·E·S

Lobster creels at Newhaven

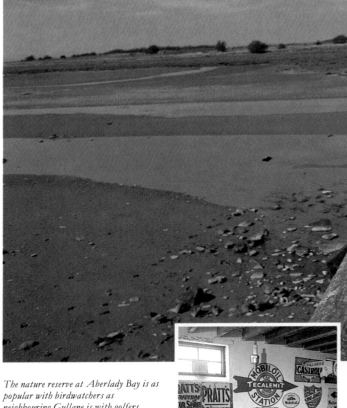

ABBOTSFORD

100 NT 5034

Sir Walter Scott was already a reasonably prosperous lawyer and a modestly successful writer when he moved from his previous country home, Ashiestiel, to the property that became Abbotsford. It was a run-down farmhouse with some land attached when he bought it in 1811. He changed its name from Cartleyhole (variously spelt and really 'clartyhole' meaning a muddy, dirty place) to Abbotsford as soon as he had set up home there. Gradually the old farmhouse was utterly transformed into the curious part-Gothic country house visited by generations of admirers. Other estates nearby were bought at the same time as the house was extended with features copied from historic edifices such as Rosslyn Chapel and Linlithgow Palace.

By 1820, rooms such as the large drawing room and the library and study added to the comfort and unique style of the property. By this time, the Waverley novels, starting with *Waverley* (1814) and followed by the *Bride of Lammermoor* and the *Legend of Montrose* were in print. In this year also, Scott was created a baronet.

Scott himself considered that Abbotsford was complete by 1825. (It included gas lighting, and was said to be the first house in Scotland to be lit by this method.) In the next year, financial disaster struck with the bankruptcy of his publishers, Ballantynes. Scott decided to earn enough by writing to pay off all debts—and he succeeded in doing this, though the labour took its toll. He died at his beloved Abbotsford in 1832, within sight and sound of the River Tweed.

The nature reserve at Aberlady Bay is as popular with birdwatchers as neighbouring Gullane is with golfers. Inset: Myreton Motor Museum is the largest of its kind in Scotland

Today, his descendants still live in the house, which retains the warm atmosphere of a much-loved home. There is much of interest to visitors, as Scott was a great collector of all kinds of Scottish artefacts: armour, a gun once belonging to Rob Roy, a sword of the Marquis of Montrose, relics of Napoleon, a silver urn presented by Byron—even the door saved from Edinburgh's Tolbooth after its demolition. Much more than a museum or shrine, Abbotsford is a living memorial to one of Scotland's greatest champions.

ABERDOUR CASTLE

98 NT 1885

The lands of Aberdour were granted to Thomas Randolph, Earl of Moray by King Robert the Bruce around 1325. Castle and lands were in turn granted to the Earls of Morton later in the 14th century. The earliest surviving part, the keep, dates from around this time. Visitors will also find later buildings of the 16th and 17th centuries and the remains of a terraced garden, bowling green and a 16th-century beehive doocot (dovecote). Nearby is the ancient St Fillan's Church, with its unusual leper window, through which lepers could join in worship.

Abbotsford House—Sir Walter Scott's last and best-loved home

ABERLADY

99NT4679

This is an attractive East Lothian village with typical red pantile-roofed cottages and a picturesque 15th-century church tower and nearby 'loupin'-on stane' (mounting block). The village's Mercat Cross is a reminder that Aberlady was once a Royal Burgh with foreign trading links as the port for Haddington, before the nearby Peffer Burn silted up in the mid-19th century. Immediately to the east is the Aberlady Bay local nature reserve, of great interest to ornithologists for its waders and wildfowl. (Casual picnickers will find easier access to sands at nearby Gullane.)

Also close by are Luffness Castle, with its 13th-century keep built on a former Norse camp, and the Myreton Motor Museum. This is a charming and wide-ranging collection of cars, commercial vehicles, cycles, military vehicles and automobilia.

BIGGAR

NT0437 (not on map)

Perhaps overlooked sometimes by visitors to Edinburgh, Biggar is easily reached and its active Museum Trust has ensured the preservation of much of interest in the town. Gladstone Court Street Museum is a varied collection of period shop-fronts and other aspects of town-life in the past, including a grocer, chemist, china merchant, ironmonger as well as

the telephone exchange, library, bank, school and many other exhibits.

Rather unexpectedly, the town is also the venue for Scotland's only preserved coal gasworks. After the town's conversion to natural gas, the works were preserved as an Ancient Monument and are now a museum, where the manufacture of coal gas is explained. There are tours and film shows, working gas lighting, a steam engine and other machinery, plus a display of gas appliances.

Greenhill Covenanters' House commemorates the Covenanters and Scotland's religious wars of the 17th century. Burn Braes Farmhouse was rescued in ruinous condition, moved and rebuilt in the town. Relics of local Covenanters are on display, as well as 17th-century furnishings and other artefacts.

BLACKNESS CASTLE

98NT0579

This was once one of Scotland's most important fortresses, built from the start for defence rather than as a residence. It dates from the 15th century and stands on a low, rocky headland which juts into the Firth of Forth. Twice burned in the 15th century, it was later used as a prison for Covenanters, then maintained by the state as a national defence (one of only four allowed by the Treaty of Union in 1707). Later it served as an ammunition depot.

BO'NESS

98NS9981

Many industries, including those based on pottery, coal, chemicals and timber (brought in through the docks which are now closed) at one time contributed to the prosperity of this town on the shores of the Forth. Now, all of them have gone. Out of the wreckage of its industrial past, Bo'ness is currently being revitalised, with an emphasis on its heritage. The Scottish Railway Preservation Society has already recreated a typical Scottish branch line with the eventual intention of rejoining the town with the main Edinburgh–Glasgow line. The nearby Birkhill Clay Mine, linked to the preserved railway, is reopening for visitors. The town's Victorian Street Fairs have proved very successful.

Nearby is Kinneil House with its 16th-century tower, which became part of the 17th-century stately home for the Dukes of Hamilton. It contains fine wall paintings and decorated ceilings. In the grounds is the outhouse in which James Watt developed the steam engine. Also in the grounds is a converted 17th-century stable block. This houses Bo'ness Museum, with displays relating to the industrial heritage of the area, as well as material from the days of the Romans. The remains of a Roman fort can be seen near by.

The romantic age of steam has been recreated in Bo'ness

CASTLE CAMPBELL

98NS9699

Castle Campbell occupies an impressive site on the shoulders of the Ochils behind the pleasant little Hillfoots town of Dollar. It offers fine views across the Forth Valley as well as walks on the open hill behind and in the wooded glen below. The fortress was once the lowland residence of the Earls of Argyll, who held high office in the Scottish court at Stirling to the west. The original 15th-century tower house on the highest point acquired a further range of buildings and a courtyard from the 16th century onwards. Historical figures associated with the castle include John Knox, who preached there, Mary, Queen of Scots who visited as a wedding guest and Cromwell, whose troops burned it in 1654.

CRICHTON CASTLE

100NT3862

Crichton Castle overlooks the valley of the infant Tyne Water amid rolling Midlothian countryside. Though the original square-towered keep is 14th-century, later courtyard extensions include an extraordinary diamond–faceted north range in Italianate style, built by the Earl of Bothwell in the 1580s, and perhaps inspired by his foreign travels.

From Crichton an attractive country walk crosses the now-vanished main railway line between Edinburgh and Carlisle, the famous Waverley Route, and continues to

Charming 16th-century houses in Culross, splendidly restored and featuring pantiled roofs and stepped gables

Borthwick, where an impressive twin-towered 15th-century tower house may be viewed from the outside.

CULROSS

98NS9885

Culross is unique in Scotland. Though other towns can claim to have preserved buildings which represent the nation's domestic architecture of the past, only in Culross is there such a strong sense of completeness in a community whose layout and appearance give a clear picture of an ordinary lowland Scottish burgh of the 17th and 18th centuries. The survival of Culross came about perhaps through economic accident. From medieval times it shared in the industrial prosperity of the Forth Valley, thanks to its plentiful supplies of coal. It had a monastery founded in 1217 and the monks were the first coal miners.

These plentiful supplies of coal allowed salt-panning to develop— the coal was used to evaporate salt water in large iron pans. Coal was also used in iron working and Culross once had a monopoly on the manufacture of iron girdles for baking! By the 16th century, the Royal Burgh of Culross was exporting great quantities of coal, salt and other Scottish products to the Low Countries of Europe, while its coal workings, owned by Sir George Bruce from 1575, were

increasing production. He invented a machine for pumping out the workings, by then well under the Firth of Forth, and built himself a grand house in the town, known locally as the Palace.

Yet Culross's fortunes were far from assured. Over the next two centuries its industries went into gradual decline—coal ran out, which affected the salt-panning and new and cheaper methods of iron working finished off its girdle manufacture. While other towns, like Bo'ness across the river, continued as manufacturing centres in the late stages of the industrial revolution, Culross slipped behind, with no civic funds for improvements such as widening streets and pulling down old property.

Right up to the 20th century, there were few changes. In 1932 the town's principal building, Sir George Bruce's Palace, was up for sale. The newly formed National Trust for Scotland was just able to buy it and start an association with the town which it retains today. After this initial purchase they gradually acquired other properties in the town—often in very poor condition. But their programme of renewal has resulted in the rehabilitation of a unique asset for the nation.

Harled and red-pantiled, the foursquare little houses scattered along the shore and up the braes now draw thousands of visitors as a showpiece—though they are still inhabited by local folk. The Palace is open to view as a wealthy merchant's house of the 17th century. It contains interesting tempera paintings. The centre of NTS activity in the town is the Town House of 1626, while another grand house is the Study of 1610. Its main room (open to view) has a 17th-century painted Norwegian ceiling.

One of the most attractive features in any stroll around are the details on many of the restored buildings—carved lintels, dates, inscribed panels and arms of guilds and craftsmen. The oldest house in the town—1577 is carved on its gable—overlooks the atmospheric Square with its cobbles and restored Mercat Cross. More than a mere film-set or museum, Culross is Scotland's best example of a community which strongly echoes the past, yet lives in the present.

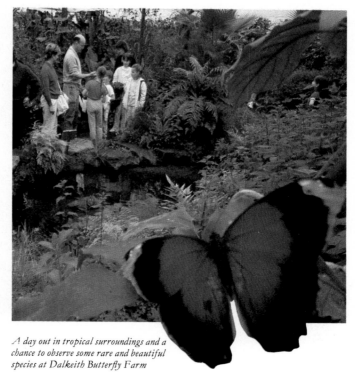

A day out in tropical surroundings and a chance to observe some rare and beautiful species at Dalkeith Butterfly Farm

DALKEITH

99NT3367
This bustling little town and route-centre close to Edinburgh has a number of attractions nearby. Dalkeith Park, in the grounds of Dalkeith Palace offers pleasant sheltered walks and a spectacular children's play area. Also near the town is Vogrie Country Park, where the walks are on a slightly larger scale through woods and parkland. The Edinburgh Butterfly Farm offers a glimpse of the tropics within easy reach of the Capital— exotic species flutter free in a spacious and lush environment. Finally, the Scottish Mining Museum is also within easy reach.

Striking sandstone ruins of Dirleton Castle

DAWYCK BOTANIC GARDENS

100NT1635
This outstation of Edinburgh's Royal Botanic Gardens set in rolling Border scenery offers tall and mature trees in variety with Far Eastern conifers forming an outstanding collection. Well-planned walks take the visitor through other fine shrubs, particularly rewarding in spring and early summer when rhododendrons provide a spectacular show. A chapel by William Burn can be seen on one of the woodland walks.

DIRLETON

99NT5183
A charming East Lothian village, with a village green slightly English in atmosphere. Dirleton's most prominent feature is its ancient castle, a 13th-century fortress which was destroyed in 1650. Within the castle grounds is a bowling green, with ancient yews and hollies around it, and an outstanding herbaceous border which makes a high summer visit particularly worthwhile. To the east, signposted from the village, is Yellowcraigs beach, giving access to a shoreline of very high quality.

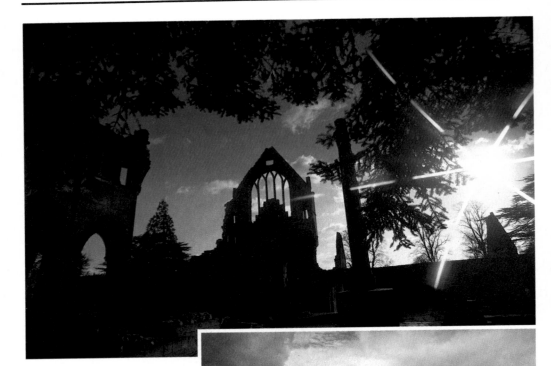

Dryburgh Abbey—presented to the nation in 1918 by Lord Glenconner. Right: The awe-inspiring Scott's View

DRYBURGH ABBEY

101 NT 5931

Dryburgh has a strong claim as the most beautiful and certainly the most peaceful of the four great Borders abbeys. Though less remains of the actual church than at Jedburgh, enough of the associated buildings and cloisters have survived to make a visit to Dryburgh a delightful experience. The abbey was founded in 1140, in the reign of King David I. Like the other abbeys it suffered badly at the hands of the English during the centuries of Border skirmishing, most notably as a result of the Earl of Hertford's raid in 1544, after which it was never rebuilt.

Sir Walter Scott is buried within the church and within easy reach is the famous 'Scott's View'— formerly his favourite stopping point for a superb vista of the River Tweed and the wooded countryside rolling out to the Eildon Hills.

DUNBAR

101 NT 6878

Dunbar is a noted seaside resort boasting exceptionally high sunshine and low rainfall figures. It is also a historic town which once commanded the main route from England to Edinburgh. Its attractions include the Victoria Harbour, used by pleasure craft as well as a mainly inshore fishery for lobster, crab and shellfish. In the early 1800s it had nearly 300 boats but later saw great decline. The harbour is overlooked by the surviving fragment of the town's greatly ruined 15th-century castle. (Kittiwakes enjoy nesting on it.) This was the castle to which Mary, Queen of Scots, retreated after the murder of Riccio—and later where she was brought after abduction by the Earl of Bothwell. Immediately eastwards, Dunbar's older Cromwell Harbour recalls its association with the military leader who defeated a superior Covenanter force here in 1650. The town has a number of interesting shop-fronts and fine Georgian buildings as well as an early 17th-century Renaissance-style Town House.

To the west lies Belhaven, with its 200-year-old brewery, and the John Muir Country Park. John Muir was born in Dunbar in 1838 and emigrated to the USA where he became a pioneer of the nature conservation movement. He was largely responsible for the establishment of the Yosemite and Sequoia National Parks. His house, marked by a plaque, is at 128 High Street. The park, named after him, offers superb beaches at Belhaven, plenty to interest birdwatchers around the estuary of the River Tyne and, further east, near Tyninghame, a choice of beach and woodland walks. Tyninghame House Gardens are open to view in the summer months (check times locally) and offer a colourful herbaceous border and peaceful wooded and terraced gardens.

Dunbar's attractions for many lie west of the town, but visitors interested in geology should not overlook the coastline east of the town where a series of lower carboniferous limestones and calciferous sandstones are exposed along the shore. These bear a variety of fossils. (The rich deposits of limestone explain the presence of a conspicuous cement factory nearby.) There is access for cars available near Barns Ness lighthouse.

DUNFERMLINE

98NT0987

Dunfermline's early history is bound up with its place as the ancient seat of the Scottish kings. Its more recent past is strongly connected to the life of its greatest son—Andrew Carnegie, millionaire philanthropist. In the long time-span between the 11th-century King Malcolm Canmore and the humble weaver who emigrated to make his fortune, Dunfermline prospered with breweries and a variety of other trades, especially linen weaving—even more particularly damask linen, for which the town was once world-renowned. Its story is told in the local museum.

Andrew Carnegie was the son of a handloom weaver. His cottage birthplace is now a museum, depicting how he made a vast fortune in the American steel business. Linked to it is a memorial hall, with further exhibits associated with him. Throughout the town there are other reminders: the Carnegie Hall, library, the Carnegie Centre, a swimming and sports centre, and the Pittencrieff Park with its acres of parkland and Pittencrieff House Museum.

All around are associations with early Scottish history. There are still traces of King Malcolm's 11th-century tower in Pittencrieff Park. On the hill above and dominating the skyline, are the remains of Dunfermline Abbey. The nave of the ancient abbey church has a much later Gothic choir, with a conspicuous tower carrying the words 'King Robert the Bruce' in stone letters. The former guest house of the Abbey, together with the monastery, lies in ruins near by. Within the grounds are the burial places of seven kings.

Falkland Palace was a source of inspiration for Sir Walter Scott

EDINBURGH CRYSTAL, PENICUIK

100NT2359

A popular attraction within sight of the Pentland Hills, Edinburgh Crystal offers visitors factory tours, a video film, shop and restaurant. On view is the whole process of producing decorative crystal pieces—glass blowing, cooling, cutting, polishing, engraving and etching.

FALKLAND PALACE

99NO2507

Dominating this picturesque village, Falkland Palace was the hunting seat of the Stuart Kings— a place for recreation and sport, rather than defence and warfare. Mary, Queen of Scots hunted deer and wild boar here and enjoyed falconry. Using the site of a much older castle, King James IV started on the new palace at the beginning of the 16th century and there were further embellishments by James V between 1525 and 1542. He died broken-hearted here on learning of the defeat of his forces by the English at Solway Moss.

Today, the palace still boasts architecture on its south range considered to be the finest of its kind anywhere in the United Kingdom, bringing a strong sense of the French Renaissance to Scotland. The Chapel Royal and King's Bedchamber have fine interiors, while the Palace Gardens in high summer are particularly colourful. Also in the gardens is the Royal Tennis Court of 1539, the oldest in Britain.

Pittencrieff Park—presented to Dunfermline by Andrew Carnegie

FIFE—THE EAST NEUK VILLAGES

99NO5603

The East Neuk (or corner) of Fife has an instantly recognisable personality of its own: inland, gently rolling fields of grain, with scattered woodlands and lush hedgerows; at the coast, the charms of the East Neuk villages—Crail, Anstruther, Pittenweem, St Monans and Elie. Each offers a different experience to the visitor, though all are bound up with the sea.

Crail is furthest east and nearest Fife Ness at the tip of Fife, the windy haunt of birdwatchers in migration time. Its picturesque harbour is still used mainly by crab and lobster boats, while its houses show the characteristic East Neuk architecture, Dutch-influenced with crow-stepped gables and red pantiled roofs. Crail also reveals its medieval trading links with the Low Countries in the Dutch style of its town house—complete with 16th-century bell and weathercock in the shape of a fish. The town's Museum and Heritage Centre tell the story of this fascinating old Royal Burgh.

Further west is Anstruther, whose harbour is on a larger scale. Boat trips leave from here for the Isle of May in season and the little town has more of the flavour of a seaside resort, with its colourful gift shops—but perhaps its most important attraction is the Scottish Fisheries Museum. It houses a comprehensive display of one of Scotland's traditional industries, from the earliest days of sail to the most modern and highly equipped vessels of today. Atmospheric tableaux recreate the life of the fishermen in the past. An aquarium section looks at the quarry they

hunted, and there is a wide range of photographs, fishing artefacts and models. There are some preserved vessels to view actually still afloat in the harbour just opposite the museum and the North Carr lightship is also nearby.

Pittenweem to the west has all the atmosphere of a working fishing harbour. Once again, the neat, white-washed, crowstepped houses are picturesque. Just off the main street is the site of a 9th-century cave-shrine of St Fillan. Inland is Kellie Castle. Also near by—rather unexpectedly—is the Lochty Steam Railway (check times locally).

St Monans, to the west, has another busy harbour and a distinctive fishermen's kirk. Founded around 1265 and dedicated to St Monan, it is separated from the rocky shoreline only by a protecting wall. Elie, whose sheltered harbour is much appreciated by dinghy and sailboard enthusiasts.

Though perhaps not strictly on the East Neuk, on the western end of Largo Bay is Largo itself, the original home of Alexander Selkirk, Defoe's *Robinson Crusoe*.

FIFE FOLK MUSEUM, CERES

99NO4011

The village of Ceres houses a comprehensive local folk museum in a 17th-century tolbooth and weigh house. Local crafts and agricultural practices, furnishing and tools of the various trades are all presented in a lively and entertaining way. In the village (at the end of the High Street), visitors should also look out for the statue of 'The Provost' a late 18th-century carving which caricatures a local ecclesiastic.

GALASHIELS

100NT4936

'Gala' has much to offer the visitor looking for a choice in quality woollens—tartans, tweed, mohair or cashmere. A leading town in the early development of the Borders' textile industry, it still has active manufacturing today and there are mill tours for visitors. The story of Galashiels is told in the Peter Anderson Woollen Mill, in the Nether Mill. The world-famous Scottish College of Textiles is also to be found in the town.

GIFFORD

99NT5368

Gifford is peacefully sited amongst very attractive wooded country on the edge of the Lammermuirs. It is an early planned village of the 17th century built on the Yester estates, which were themselves once owned by the de Giffords, a prominent Norman family. Their ancient castle (in the grounds of the much later Yester House by William Adam), now almost completely ruined, was the site of the original Goblin Hall, a subterranean great hall or pit, described in Scott's *Marmion*. In the village can be seen the 1780 Mercat Cross, a fine town house with Victorian clock tower and the church of 1710. There is a picturesque lime tree avenue leading to Yester House nearby.

GULLANE

99NT4882

Bracing sea air and pleasant coastal walking is on offer at prosperous-looking Gullane, seemingly surrounded by golf courses. The settlement was extended in Victorian times by the construction of large mansions within easy commuting distance of Edinburgh and Gullane soon became established as a golfing resort. In the 17th century, church and village were overwhelmed by sand. In this century, the popularity of Gullane's golden sandy crescent needed remedial action by the local authority to protect and stabilise its dune system to prevent any kind of a repetition.

Gifford's picturesque 18th-century church. Opposite: Taking a closer look at the workings of Nether Mill, Galashiels. Inset 1: Colourful cones of wool. Inset 2: An apt motto

HADDINGTON

99 NT 5174

The former county town of East Lothian, Haddington has its origins as a Royal Burgh in the 12th century. The town centre streets form an unusual thin triangular shape which still recalls the original layout of the town. By the 16th century, the area within the triangle was built over. Later, fine 18th- and early 19th-century buildings were erected. Many of these survive today and Haddington has well over a hundred buildings listed of architectural or historic interest.

The most conspicuous of these is perhaps the Town House, originally by William Adam in 1748, with later additions including an early 19th-century steeple. The town's nearby High Street is a remarkable survival, showing unity in its elevations and shop-fronts — and a cheerful outbreak of harmonious colours, as a result of a co-ordinated painting scheme.

Among the town's many notable buildings are Poldrate Mill, cleverly converted into an arts and community centre, Haddington House, with its restored 17th-century garden and St Mary's Parish Church, dating from the 14th and 15th centuries. In a separate building behind the splendid Corinthian decoration of 18th-century Carlyle House, is the Jane Welsh Carlyle Museum. Wife of writer and man of letters Thomas Carlyle, Jane Welsh was born in the house — which features a period drawing room and exhibits associated with the Carlyles and their circle.

Just a mile south of the town is Lennoxlove House, home of the Duke and Duchess of Hamilton. Fine portraits and furniture as well as artefacts relating to Mary, Queen of Scots are on display.

HAWICK

100 NT 5014

Hawick is the largest of the Borders towns, with a range of light industry as well as its agricultural activities and, naturally, woollen mills. Like the other Borders towns, rugby has a great following here and the tradition of the Common Riding is also very strong. Wilton Park, a sheltered and colourful riverside park with its own leisure facilities, is the site of the Hawick Museum which houses a wide-ranging collection of local artefacts relating to the area's natural and industrial heritage.

HILLFOOTS TOWNS

98 NS 9099

This is the collective name for the string of settlements running along the south side of the Ochils, north of the River Forth. The streams running off the steep scarp face of the hills provided power for mills, while their open, grassy slopes provided pasture for sheep and hence wool. Though smaller in scale and area, this created in turn another of Scotland's knitwear areas, second in size only to the Borders.

West of the M90, Rumbling Bridge offers woodland walks to view the scenic gorge cut by melt-water after the last Ice Age. The peaceful and well-kept little town of Dollar has some mill buildings remaining from past textile activities but its chief attraction is its glen leading up to Castle Campbell. Further west, Tillicoultry offers exploration of the Ochils on foot via the Mill Glen (just east of the quarry).

Between Tillicoultry and Alva is the Ochil Hills Woodland Park, created on the former policies of the now vanished Alva House. More woodland walks can be enjoyed—and further expeditions into the Ochils via the Silver Glen—a name which recalls how the Erskine family, the original owners of Alva House, made their fortune from local silver mining in the early 18th century. Conspicuous above Alva itself is the distinctive architecture of Strude Mill, built in 1827. This is the largest of what was once a complex of mill buildings whose water supply arrangements can be seen where Alva Glen opens out above the town. This is an area of great interest to the industrial archaeologist. Continuing westwards, the Ochils run towards Stirling via Menstrie with its 16th-century restored castle. Stirling is easily reached, and offers a great number of attractions to the visitor.

Full information on local mills and shops is obtainable from the Mill Heritage Centre at the Clock Mill, Tillicoultry.

HILL OF TARVIT HOUSE

99 NO3811
Within easy reach of the bustling little town of Cupar, this fine Edwardian country house was built on the site of an older dwelling and remodelled and designed by Sir Edward Lorimer. Beautiful furnishings and fittings are on display, as well as a pleasant garden on the slopes above. There is also a walk to a viewpoint.

THE HIRSEL

101 NT8240
Though on the edge of 'day-tripping' from Edinburgh, nevertheless Coldstream is the first Scottish town over the Border via the A697, a most attractive way in to Scotland. Thus one of the country's first attractions for visitors from the south is the Hirsel, home of the Douglas Homes. The Hirsel House is private, but this Borders estate welcomes visitors to its grounds at all times of the year. There is a museum and craft centre in old farmstead buildings with displays on the work of the estate. The varied habitat of woodland, field, parkland and loch is of particular interest to birdwatchers, while the estate's Dundock Wood offers a magnificent rhododendron display.

INCHCOLM ABBEY

98 NT1882
The island position of this abbey, founded about 1132 by King Alexander I, has no doubt contributed to the well-preserved state of its monastic buildings, which include church, chapter house and cloister. Check in Aberdour and South Queensferry for details of boat trips.

Main picture: 16th-century bridge over the River Tyne, Haddington. Inset left: Nova Scotia Exhibition Room, Menstrie Castle. Inset right: On sale at the Clock Mill, Tillicoultry

Above: Colour-washed houses overlook the Market Square in Jedburgh. Inset: River Tweed meanders into Kelso. Opposite: The elegant Kellie Castle boasts an equally fine interior

JEDBURGH

101 NT6520

A 'gateway' town on the A68, Jedburgh suffered much in the past through being within a day's march of the English Border. Its abbey is said to have been burned nine times by English armies and eight times rebuilt, till the last occasion when it was severely damaged, along with the other Borders abbeys, during the Earl of Hertford's campaign—the 'rough wooing' of the young Mary, Queen of Scots.

Scotland's tragic queen has strong associations with the town, recalled in displays in Queen Mary's House. This is a rare example of a fortified Borders house, in which, some say, Mary lodged in 1566. Much older are the ruins of Jedburgh Abbey, dating from around 1118. Its story and that of the Augustinian canons is told in a nearby visitor centre. Many other historic buildings survive in the town, including the Castle Jail, a Georgian building on the site of Jedburgh's long-vanished castle. It is now a museum. There is an interesting town trail to follow—Bonnie Prince Charlie's House, the County Buildings (on the site of the courthouse where the young Sir Walter Scott first appeared as an advocate) and the 16th-century Canongate Bridge are just a few of the historic places on the short walking tour.

KELLIE CASTLE

99 NO5205

A castle with a convoluted history, amid the barley fields of East Fife, Kellie Castle was restored by Professor James Lorimer in Victorian times. This started an association with his descendants and this ancient seat which lasts to the present day. Visitors will see fine 16th- and 17th-century architecture, beautifully remodelled interiors and a charming and secluded walled garden.

KELSO

101 NT7333

A particularly picturesque Border town, Kelso is unusual in its town centre layout—a wide cobbled square which lends a Continental flavour. The town stands at the meeting place of the Rivers Teviot and Tweed and its rather grand five-arch bridge was built in 1805 by Rennie, it is said, as a model for London Bridge.

Within a moment's walk of the town centre is the magnificent fragment of Kelso Abbey, founded by David I in 1128. Though once the largest of the Borders abbeys, like the others it was damaged—in fact, almost totally destroyed—by the Earl of Hertford under orders from King Henry VIII of England. The abbey's garrison of 100 men and 12 monks was also slaughtered. Built to a plan unique in Scotland, its surviving tower is part of the original work.

Kelso is associated with the estate of the Duke of Roxburghe whose Floors Castle is conspicuous on the edge of town. Visitors should not, however, try to visit the original town of Roxburgh—it fell into decay in the 15th century—having been sacked and burned by invading English armies repeatedly over the centuries. It stood on the south bank of the Tweed, overlooking the Kelso of today. Only a ruined castle and a few grassy mounds survive, though a village three miles away retains the name. Visitors can, however, visit Floors Castle, an impressive William Adam mansion (1721), later embellished with domes, spires and turrets by William Playfair in 1841. It is said to be the largest inhabited house in Scotland.

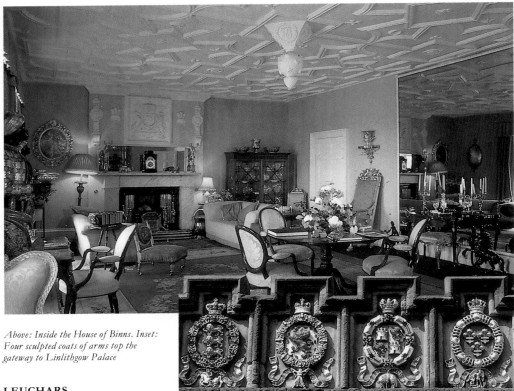

Above: Inside the House of Binns. Inset: Four sculpted coats of arms top the gateway to Linlithgow Palace

LEUCHARS

99NO4521

Not just a little village on the end of an active air base, Leuchars has its own range of items of interest. These include Leuchars Norman Church, reckoned to be a fragment of the very finest Norman architecture to be seen anywhere in the United Kingdom. The architecture of the chancel and apse have remained virtually unchanged for seven centuries. Matching this 12th-century craftsmanship is a 17th-century belltower.

Earlshall Castle near by was visited by Mary, Queen of Scots in 1561, when it was only a few years old. Sir Robert Lorimer restored it in 1891 and the castle is now famous for its painted ceiling, broadsword collection and extraordinary topiary in the shape of chess pieces. Beyond Leuchars is access to Tentsmuir Beach, a superb sandy beach backed by extensive coniferous plantings, offering walks in all seasons and birdlife in variety.

LINLITHGOW

98NS9977

Linlithgow grew around the royal manor house originally built by King David I in the 12th century. On its site, James I later built Linlithgow Palace. Work started in 1425, and continued under subsequent Stuart kings. Thus Linlithgow town was bound up with the fortunes of one of Scotland's principal royal residences. It enjoyed a time of great prosperity till the Union of the Crowns in 1603 after which Linlithgow Palace fell into disuse. About the same time, ports on the Forth, particularly Bo'ness and Queensferry, were developed and took trade away from the town.

Afterwards it turned to cloth-making, tanning and shoemaking, among other activities. The former life and trades of the town are remembered in the annual 'Riding of the Marches' while those old parts of the High Street and main square which have survived the developers are now a preservation area and form a Heritage Trail for visitors. The town's dominating feature is still its palace and church. Linlithgow Palace is only a shell, with neither roof, wooden floors nor any furnishings. These were destroyed by fire after the Hanoverian General Hawley, defeated by Bonnie Prince Charlie at Falkirk, occupied Linlithgow Palace. His dragoons accidentally set it alight. Yet this square courtyard surrounded by four ranges of buildings still retains the atmosphere of a Royal residence. Mary, Queen of Scots was born here in 1542 and it was her father who essentially completed the Palace, except for the reconstruction of the north wing carried out by her son, James VI in 1618–20.

Just south of the Palace and topped with its controversial modern 'crown of thorns' spire is the ancient St Michael's Church, mainly 15th-century. In spite of much destruction during the Reformation, St Michael's image uniquely survives within the church, which has been extensively restored.

There are several places of interest near the town. Excursions by canal boat are available on the Union Canal and there is a canal museum, housed in former stables for the towing horses. A few minutes south of the town is Beecraigs Country Park, 700 acres, whose attractions include stocked trout fishing, a red deer farm, visitor centre, a variety of walks and trails and some fine views across the Forth Valley. There are other country parks in the area including Muiravonside, to the west, with woodland walks, relics of former industry and the recreation of a typical lowland Scottish farm of the 19th century. Polkemmet and Almondell Country Parks lie further south. Cairnpapple Hill offers fine views and is an important early burial site, now excavated and a scheduled Ancient Monument. Also within easy reach is Torphichen Preceptory, once the Scottish 'headquarters' of the Knights of St John of Jerusalem.

North-east of the town is the House of the Binns. It was built by Thomas Dalyell in the first half of the 17th century. His son 'General Tam' was a fervent Royalist— captured at Worcester by Cromwell's troops he escaped the Tower of London, fled abroad and lead an adventurous life till the Restoration. He returned and afterwards defeated a Covenanting army at Rullion Green. There are many stories that he was in league with the Devil. On the shore is Blackness Castle.

LOCH LEVEN

98NO1502
A major Lowland loch within easy reach of Edinburgh by the M90, Loch Leven is famed for the quality of its fishing and also as a wintering ground for spectacular numbers of wildfowl. The Royal Society for the Protection of Birds has a major visitor centre on the south shore of the loch with excellent viewing

facilities and displays on the natural history and ecology of the loch. A nature trail leading up the hill behind the centre gives further excellent views.

The loch's most famous historical attraction is Loch Leven Castle, an island fortress accessible by boat from nearby Kinross. It consists of an uncompromisingly square tower house dating from the early 14th century and a walled courtyard of no great thickness— its island position being its best defence. Mary, Queen of Scots was held captive here in 1567 before escaping to defeat in battle and exile across the Border. The nearby town of Kinross has an interesting museum and offers variety in shopping, including knitwear. There is another ruined tower house, Burleigh Castle, north-east of the town.

LOCHORE MEADOWS

98NT1696
Claiming to be the largest reclamation scheme anywhere in Britain, Lochore Meadows Country Park is now attractive green countryside with loch, nature reserve and golf course. When the last pit closed in the area in 1967 it left only ugly spoil-heaps (bings), acres of slurry, rows of poor housing—and all the industrial dereliction of a worn-out coalfield.

For the next eight years bulldozers and earthmoving equipment regraded and

Loch Leven—once prison for a queen, now an important nature reserve

landscaped over 15 million cubic feet of pit waste. Two hundred thousand trees have been planted. The parkland even has a Countryside Ranger Service to help visitors who come to fish, walk, sail or otherwise enjoy this recreated countryside in the centre of Fife.

MANDERSTON HOUSE

101NT8154
Manderston claims to be the finest Edwardian country house in Britain. It has also been described as the 'swansong' of the country house and features a unique silver staircase, elegant public rooms and sophisticated 'below stairs' arrangements, as well as nearly 60 acres of gardens. Nearby is Duns, a former county town and the centre of the fine agricultural area of the Merse.

Manderston House Gardens

It is possible to board many of the aircraft at the Museum of Flight

bottleneck has also recently opened.) The Romans occupied the area and there is evidence of very early settlement around this estuary site.

The town gained its reputation as the 'Honest Toun' in 1332 when the townsfolk protected the Regent Randolph after he fell ill on his way through the town. Though he later died, his successor as Regent, the Earl of Mar, gave Musselburgh this accolade, which it keeps to this day and remembers in its annual Honest Toun celebrations, much in the style of the Borders' Common Ridings.

The town has an old tolbooth and town house and, within the grounds of Loretto School, stands Pinkie House, a 17th-century building with a painted gallery and decorative plaster ceilings (check opening times locally). Picturesque Inveresk is a leafy residential area just south of the main part of the town. The gardens of 17th-century Inveresk House are open to view, with shrubs and climbing roses particularly notable.

MELLERSTAIN

101 NT6439
One of Scotland's great Georgian Houses, Mellerstain is a fine example of the work of the Adam family—begun in the 1720s by William and completed by his son Robert in the 1770s. It contains superb plasterwork and other decoration as well as a notable art collection and outstanding 18th-century furniture. There are also attractive Italian gardens and a lake. (Check opening times locally).

MELROSE

100 NT5433
Melrose Abbey helps draw visitors to this peaceful little Borders town by the Eildon Hills. King David I brought Cistercians to Melrose from Rievaulx in Yorkshire in 1136. These monks laid out a monastery and then the abbey kirk amid fertile fields. Amongst other agricultural activities they traded in wool, creating the foundation of the Borders industry. Like the other Borders abbeys, Melrose was repeatedly sacked and burned. The ruins today date from the 14th and 15th centuries. Excavations have uncovered the layout of many of the monastic buildings, and the fine traceried stonework of the nave and choir can still be seen. There is a museum at the entrance displaying fascinating artefacts found on the site.

Immediately adjacent is Priorwood Gardens, a pleasant walled garden specialising in herbaceous plants, particularly those which can be dried and preserved. Fruit growers will be interested in the garden's collection of old apple varieties. Another attraction near by is the Melrose Motor Museum, a private collection featuring not only full-size vintage vehicles, but toy cars, as well as old signs and other automobilia. Finally, above the town, the distinctive profile of the Eildon Hills (*Trimontium* to the Romans) is a landmark for miles around offering attractive walking and superb views of the Borders countryside.

MUSEUM OF FLIGHT, EAST FORTUNE

99 NT5478
At East Fortune (meaning fort-toun, referring to settlement near a fort) a World War II airfield houses a varied collection of historic aircraft, ranging from a Spitfire to a Comet. Other historical displays include information on the R34, which flew from the East Fortune field to New York and back in 1919. (Check opening times locally.)

MUSSELBURGH

99 NT3472
Though within easy commuting distance of Edinburgh, the distinct community of Musselburgh, for administrative purposes, is in East Lothian. It is of former strategic importance as the main bridging point of the River Esk. An early bridge survives here, bypassed by Rennie's bridge of 1807. (A complete bypass of the town's

NORTH BERWICK

99NT5485

This attractive and prosperous little resort town, popular with Edinburgh day-trippers, has fine sandy beaches, a sailing harbour, outdoor swimming pool and parks. It also offers interesting shopping and a coastline worth exploring on both sides of the town. Behind is the cone of the Berwick Law (613ft/187m). It is the plug of an ancient volcano, of a hard igneous rock known to geologists as trachyte, which now rises out of the sandstones of the coastal plain.

Though steep-sided and dramatic, there is a good path to the top from a car park south of the town.

Boat excursions round the Bass Rock leave from North Berwick. Like the Berwick Law, this spectacular island crag is another volcanic plug. It is famed for its huge gannet colony (approximately 14,000 pairs) and the bird's scientific name *Sula bassana* even refers to this rock. The Bass is three miles from North Berwick, two miles from the coast at Tantallon Castle, 340ft high (100m) and about a mile in circumference. The first historical mention of its gannets was in 1493 and later King James IV passed a piece of early conservation legislation protecting them in 1581. The Rock has served as a prison and barracks, with fortifications appearing on it as early as the 11th century, though St Baldred had a hermitage here around the 8th century. The Rock became a state prison in 1671 and four Jacobite prisoners turned the tables on their guards, holding the Bass from 1691 to 1694.

North Berwick with its attractive harbour offering ferry trips to the Bass Rock, is a popular tourist spot

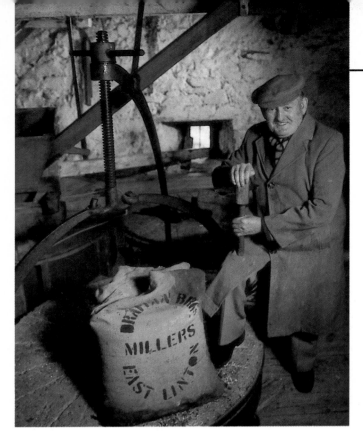

Preston Mill in action

aspect of old-time rural life. This home for 500 nesting pigeons once supplied winter meat for the local laird. Also near East Linton is the Rennie Memorial, commemorating the engineer John Rennie, designer of London's Waterloo Bridge (and many others) who was born on the farm at Phantassie.

ROSSLYN CHAPEL

100 NT2763
Signposted in the village of Roslin and overlooking the woodlands of Roslin Glen, Rosslyn Chapel is an extraordinary work in stone. Founded by Sir William St Clair, its 15th-century carving, which includes the magnificently ornate Prentice Pillar, draws many visitors. It achieved fame as long ago as 1805 following the publication of Sir Walter Scott's *The Lay of the Last Minstrel*. Part of the setting is the chapel and nearby Rosslyn Castle (not open to the public). In addition to some 'unofficial' woodland walks around Roslin Glen, the steep valley of the North Esk, the attractive aspects of Midlothian's countryside can be discovered by following the railway walkway west of Rosewell towards Auchendinny and Penicuik. This was one of a number of local lines engineered by Sir Thomas Bouch—who constructed the infamous first Tay Bridge.

ST ABBS HEAD

101 NT9169
This nature reserve offers dramatic cliff-top walking and superb coastal scenery. There is limited parking at times near the lighthouse which is itself near the most spectacular of the seabird colonies. Guillemots, razorbills and kittiwakes are among the commonest species thronging the cliff ledges, with shags and cormorants lower down. There are also other gull species and some puffins. Estimated total numbers in this high-rise 'bird city' are thought to be around 50,000. On the landward side of the 300ft (90m) high cliffs are grassy slopes, scrub and a sheltered loch making St Abbs Head a rewarding spot at bird migration time. The waters offshore are also protected as Scotland's first voluntary Marine Reserve.

PEEBLES

101 NT2540
'Peebles for Pleasure' is a motto still current, judging by the continuing popularity of this pleasant little town with visitors from Edinburgh. Its curious name may relate to Welsh 'pebyll' meaning tents. Though its dwellings became permanent enough to give it Royal Burgh status in 1367, like so many other parts of the Borders it lay too often in the path of marauding forces. The town has a very picturesque setting in the hills and the varied building styles along the broad main streets offer plenty of shops to attract the browser. Peebles also has a local museum and is associated with the Chambers brothers, Robert and William (of Encyclopedia and Dictionaries fame) who were born in the town in the beginning of the 19th century. A relic of early times is the ruin of the Cross Kirk, originally founded in the 13th century.

There is a choice of walks and the parkland bordering the River Tweed is popular. The Glentress Forest, east of the town, offers a variety of routes. Within easy walking distance of the town, west along the pleasant river banks, is Neidpath Castle (also accessible by car from the A72). It still has the air of a medieval keep and was associated with the Frasers and later the Hays of Yester. A later Lord Yester supported Charles II and consequently was besieged here by Cromwell.

East of the town is the estate of Kailzie with its mature woodland and a wild garden.

THE PENTLAND HILLS

98 NT1258
Even an enthusiast like Sir Walter Scott remarked that the Pentland Hills are 'neither rocky nor highly elevated' yet they hold a special place as the Capital's own hills— 'the hills of home' as R L Stevenson wrote from far Samoa. They are the city's recreation area with easy access at a number of points, starting at Fairmilehead near the ski-slope. On the north-facing slopes of the Pentlands, another popular starting place for walking excursions is at Bonaly, south of Colinton. To the south, Flotterstone on the A702 gives easy walking, along the Glencorse Reservoir access road. On the near, or Edinburgh, side of Silverburn, roadside parking gives access to a path through to Balerno as well as walks to the nearby tops including the extensively cairned Carnethy Hill, with fine views across Midlothian to the Moorfoots. Finally, Nine Mile Burn is yet another starting point with signposted routes on to the windy grasslands, also within easy reach of the city.

PRESTON MILL

99 NT5978
This picturesque water mill, much photographed and painted, is an almost unique example of a building which once had a vital role in the agricultural community. Its sophisticated gear-driven water-powered machinery is in working order and open to visitors. Near by is Phantassie Doocot, another

ST ANDREWS

99NO5016

The old ecclesiastical capital of Scotland, St Andrews is also associated with Scotland's oldest university, and closely linked to the story of golf in Scotland. Added to this curious mix is a range of shopping extraordinary for a town of its size, and some fine architecture, including the most unusual survival of a town gate. The original street layout of the medieval town still remains and is well seen from the top of the 12th-century St Rule's Tower (108ft/34m). It stands next to the ruined cathedral which was the largest religious building ever constructed in Scotland.

The religious quest for knowledge prompted the founding of the university in the early 15th century. Teaching had begun about four decades before St Salvator's College was founded in 1450 by Archbishop Kennedy. Another important relic of the past is St Andrews Castle, once the palace of the archbishops and now in rocky ruin above the sea. There is also a unique reminder of its stormy history of siege, martyrdom and murder—a mine and counter-mine open to the public (or those who dare!).

A choice of golf courses, including the famous Old Course, lies north of the town on what was once short, rabbit-cropped turf by the sea's edge—the place where the game began, though this is hotly disputed by other east coast communities. St Andrews also has fine beaches and coastal walking. The town's history can be explored in the Museum of the St Andrews Preservation Trust. Visitors should also find the Botanic Gardens, sometimes missed because of the other town centre attractions.

THE SCOTTISH MINING MUSEUM, NEWTONGRANGE

100NT3363

Though Scotland is associated with fine scenery and wild country, its National Mining Museum at Newtongrange in Midlothian and Prestongrange in East Lothian is an important reminder of the other face of Scotland and its industrial heritage.

The museum is in two places, with the most extensive visitor

Mechanics of mining explained at Newtongrange

St Andrews Cathedral

facilities being at Newtongrange in the former Lady Victoria Colliery. This pit, finally closed in 1981, was sunk between 1890 and 1894 and was for long a 'model' pit in the industry. It was run by the Lothian Coal Company on lands owned by the Marquis of Lothian. Adjacent to the pit, extensive accommodation for mining families was built, in effect the complete village of Newtongrange. The visitor centre, in what was once the wages office of the pit, features tableaux which tell the story of a day in the life of an ordinary miner and how the managers of the mine had a complete hold over their employees—owning their houses and even the village pub! In addition to visiting the

interpretative centre, visitors can put on 'hard hats' and tour other parts of the pit complex. (There are no trips actually underground available, as the main shaft was sealed after pit closure.)

Lady Victoria offers its visitors a day out with a difference and encourages exploration of a route which is a little away from the usual tourist trails. This is the Coal Heritage Trail running from Newtongrange via Newbattle.

Finally, between Prestonpans and Musselburgh is Prestongrange. On this site, the monks of Newbattle Abbey opened what is thought to be the first British coalmine, some time before AD1200. A colliery closed here as recently as 1962. Its giant beam engine is a conspicuous monument to vanished industry, recalled in an audio-visual show and exhibition of various mining artefacts.

SCOTTISH MUSEUM OF WOOLLEN TEXTILES, WALKERBURN

100NT3637

In Walkerburn, a little community on the Tweed founded on its textile industry, the visitor will find the Scottish Museum of Woollen Textiles on the premises of a major knitwear company. It tells the story of the industry from its earliest days with hand spinning through the gradual introduction of mechanisation to the modern methods of today. There are tableaux, artefacts, models, and information on natural dyes, knitting patterns, shearing and all aspects of the woollen trade—as well as a knitwear shop. Walkerburn itself is also a centre for fishing and local walks.

The River Forth is crossed in parallel by an elegant Victorian rail bridge and a sleek 1960's road bridge. Inset: Dalmeny House

SELKIRK

100 NT4728
An attractive little town on the River Ettrick, with its textile mills in the river valley, Selkirk is the original home of the Selkirk Bannock, a delicious fruit loaf or bun, available locally and in other Borders towns. The courtroom used by Sir Walter Scott while he was sheriff here can still be seen. Halliwell's House, in a row of 18th-century dwelling houses near the town centre, tells the story of this community, as well as of the building's own link with the ironmongery trade, in a small museum.

West of the town is another of the area's stately homes, Bowhill. Inside the Georgian-style house, begun in 1812, there is an outstanding painting collection as well as fine furniture and porcelain. Out of doors, visitors can enjoy the woodlands, garden and nature trails.

SMAILHOLM TOWER

101 NT6334
Smailholm Tower stands gaunt and windswept, in open country with an outstanding view on all sides. It is a fine example of a 16th-century Border peel tower. It houses a small exhibition on the theme of Scott's *Minstrelsy of the Scottish Border*. Near by Sandyknowe Farm was often visited by Scott in boyhood, as it was the home of his grandfather.

SOUTH QUEENSFERRY

98 NT1278
This picturesque little town in the shadow of the Forth Bridges was once a royal burgh of importance at the southern end of the ferry link across the Forth estuary. This role stretched back to the 11th-century Queen Margaret, who initiated a ferry here for the benefit of pilgrims from the south who were visiting Dunfermline, royal seat and abbey. The ferry service ended only in 1964 with the opening of the Forth Road Bridge. The original settlement with its main street running along the shore still has some interesting architecture including the Hawes Inn (1683), which features in R L Stevenson's *Kidnapped*, and other 17th-century town houses as well as a church and tolbooth.

Two stately homes lie close by. The estate of Dalmeny lies between the edge of South Queensferry and the west shore of the River Almond at Cramond. (There is a coastal walk accessible to visitors by a little ferry at Cramond.) Dalmeny House is the seat of the Earls of Rosebery. It was built in a Tudor Gothic style in 1815. Within the house is a fine collection of paintings, furniture, tapestries and works of art. These are from two collections: the Rosebery collection, which relates to the political, historical and artistic life of the Roseberys, and the Mentmore Collection, brought to Dalmeny before the famous Mentmore sale in 1977.

Upstream from the great bridges, the other attraction for visitors is the extra-sumptuous Hopetoun House, the ancestral home of the Marquess of Linlithgow. The 1st Earl of Hopetoun commissioned the architect Sir William Bruce, to build a great mansion, completed in 1703. Subsequently the Adam family, firstly William from 1721, then his sons John and Robert, greatly extended it. They were also responsible for many of the interiors which are still intact and seen by visitors today, amid many other treasures—paintings, china, costumes, decorations. There are also extensive gardens.

THIRLESTANE CASTLE

100 NT5348

From a tower built in the late 16th century, Thirlestane Castle was gradually extended over the following centuries. This imposing mansion of towers and turrets has been the home of the Maitland family for four centuries. Thirlestane today offers the visitor interesting interiors, particularly in its state rooms, with beautiful plaster ceilings and panelling.

In the grounds of the castle is the Borders Country Life Museum, which tells the story of the area's rural life, agriculture and land use from prehistoric times to the present day by means of exhibitions and displays as well as a programme of talks and demonstrations.

Borders Country Life Museum

TANTALLON CASTLE

99 NT6084

This 14th-century stronghold of the powerful Douglas family is dramatically sited on a headland overlooking the sea and the Bass Rock. It presents an impressive curtain wall to the south and offers visitors fine—if slightly dizzying—views seawards and across the East Lothian countryside. With its spectacularly defensive site, it was virtually impregnable till finally taken by General Monk in 1651.

Seat of the Earls of Lauderdale, Thirlestane Castle is one of the grandest of the Borders castles

TRAQUAIR HOUSE

100 NT3335

Traquair claims to be the oldest continually inhabited house in Scotland and has been visited by 27 Scottish or English monarchs since 1107. It is also associated with Mary, Queen of Scots—her second cousin, the 4th Earl of Traquair, Sir John Stuart, was Captain of her bodyguard. (She visited Traquair during a hunt in 1566, just after the birth of her son, the future James VI.) A number of relics associated with her can be seen, along with interesting furniture, porcelain, miniatures and embroidery.

The 5th Earl of Traquair was visited by Bonnie Prince Charlie during the last Jacobite uprising. After the Prince's departure, he closed the famous Bear Gates, swearing they would not be opened till a Stuart returned to the throne. They remain closed to this day. The house itself has changed little since the 17th century, though its main tower is much older. In addition to the historic interiors, today's visitors can enjoy woodland walks and craft workshops—and a genuine 18th-century alehouse in which the present owners, the Maxwell Stuarts, brew and sell to the public their own (very strong!) Traquair Ale.

MAPS & DRIVES

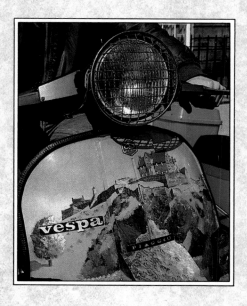

*An Edinburgh youth displays a pride in his city –
combined with a certain artistic talent*

Tweed Valley and Moorfoot Hills

A short drive in any direction out of Edinburgh leads to either sea or countryside that seems a million miles in atmosphere from this cosmopolitan city. This southerly route is no exception. First, there is Roslin, a sleepy mining village in the shadow of the Pentland Hills, with more than one tale to fascinate any visitor to its Chapel and its creepy Castle hidden in the woody depths of Roslin Glen. The River Esk flows southward from here through some spectacular open moorland to Gladhouse Reservoir and beyond to the majestic Moorfoot Hills. Further south is the green and pleasant valley of the River Tweed whose waters turn the great wheels of the textile mills that make Peebles a famous former county town. The return journey takes in Scotland's oldest inhabited house, Traquair House.

Shops filled with high-quality woollens are irresistible to visitors to Peebles main street

From Edinburgh city centre follow the Galashiels signs through the suburbs to leave by the A7. After some 2 miles at the roundabout take 2nd exit, then in ¼ mile go forward on to the A701, signed Peebles. Later continue through Straiton and on to Bilston. Here turn left on to the B7006, signed Roslin. The drive soon enters the former mining village of **Roslin**. Of interest here is the richly decorated 15th-century Rosslyn Chapel — the centrepiece of which is the magnificently carved Prentice Pillar.

At Roslin turn right (for the Chapel keep forward). In ¼mile turn left, signed Rosewell, and descend (16%) — passing the turning to Roslin Glen (on the right). Cross the River Esk and in 1¼miles bear right. At the T-junction in **Rosewell** *turn right on to the A6094 (no sign). Two miles further branch left on to an unclassified road, signed Gladhouse Reservoir, and cross Cauldhall Moor.* Rolling countryside is dominated by the Moorfoot Hills ahead.

In 1½ miles turn left on to the B6372 (still signed Gladhouse) and after another 1½ miles turn right unclassified (no sign). [In 1¼ miles a short detour to the left may be taken to view the **Gladhouse Reservoir**.] *Continue forward for 3 miles, then descend before turning left onto the Peebles road, A703, to follow the valley of the Eddleston Water. At the village of Eddleston turn right, unclassified, signed Lyne via Meldons. A gradual ascent is then made to reach 900ft (274m) among the twin Meldon peaks. Descend and in 1¼ miles bear left. On reaching the main road turn left, A72 (no sign). Continue alongside the River Tweed and after 2¼ miles to the right stands the 14th-century stronghold of* **Neidpath Castle.** The castle walls, 11-feet thick in places, were bombarded by Cromwell's artillery.

One mile further enter the town of **Peebles.** Peebles is a popular inland resort and angling centre. Some 2½ miles to the south-east are the extensive grounds of **Kailzie Gardens.** *Remain on the A72, signed Galashiels, and continue to follow the Tweed valley to* **Innerleithen** — a woollen manufacturing town and former spa. A short distance to the south is **Traquair House,** Scotland's oldest inhabited house which dates back to the 10th century.

In Innerleithen turn left on to the B709, signed Heriot, and follow the valley of the Leithen Water. Later there is a climb over a narrow pass at 1250ft (381m) before descending alongside the Dewar Burn. Two miles beyond the summit go forward with the B7007, signed Gorebridge. The drive then climbs on to more high ground along the northern extremity of the Moorfoot Hills which offer many fine views.

At the junction with the A7 turn right, signed Galashiels. In 1¼ miles turn left on to the Pathhead road, B6367. In another 1¼ miles bear left and continue to **Crichton.** To the south-west of the hamlet is the 14th- to 16th- century **Crichton Castle** — notable for the Earl of Bothwell's Italianate wing.

At Crichton turn left, then right and proceed to Pathhead. Here turn left with the A68, signed Edinburgh. [In just over ¾ mile a detour to the left along the B6372 leads to the **Vogrie Estate Country Park.**]

Remain on the A68 to Dalkeith. Here is **Dalkeith Palace,** a mansion by Vanbrugh, built around 1700 (grounds are open to the public).

In the town turn right, then left, still signposted Edinburgh. After a further 3¾ miles on the right is the 14th-century stronghold of **Craigmillar Castle.** The castle has associations with Mary, Queen of Scots, and some 16th- and 17th-century apartments still survive. *In almost a mile, at the roundabout, take the 2nd exit and follow the City Centre signs.*

Top right: The River Tweed – a source of industry and recreation for Peebles folk

Bottom right: Colourful blooms at Kailzie Gardens

Below: Neidpath Castle enjoys a tranquil setting on the banks of the River Tweed

Almost all places in **bold type** are fully described in the Out of City and City Centre gazetters.

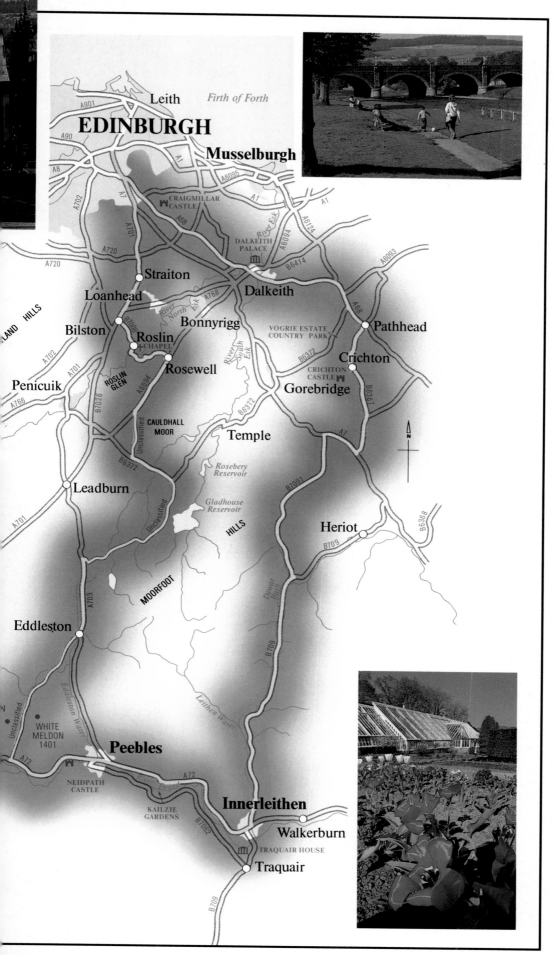

Country Parks and Stately Homes along the Forth

There are numerous country parks and stately homes in and around the city. This drive encompasses those to the west of Edinburgh beyond the airport and towards the ancient royal burgh of Linlithgow. The return journey offers some fine views of the river and its two handsome bridges.

Leave Edinburgh by following the Glasgow signs along the A8 through the western suburbs. In 3 miles, on the right, are the grounds of the **Zoological Park**. *At all the ensuing roundabouts keep forward and after some further 2¼ miles pass the turning to the* **Royal Highland Showground** *at* **Ingliston**. Also the site of the Scottish Agricultural Museum.

In 2 miles at the roundabout take the third exit on the A89, signed Bathgate. Two miles further at the next roundabout go forward and in ¾ mile pass the turning to **Almondell Country Park** *(on the left). Remain on the A89 and continue forward at all road junctions for almost 6 miles, then at the roundabout take 4th exit to reach the outskirts of* **Bathgate**. This industrial town is the commercial centre of West Lothian and was the birthplace in 1811 of Sir James Simpson — famous for his discovery of chloroform as an anaesthetic.

On entering Bathgate branch right on to the B792, signed Linlithgow. In 1 mile turn right, then left and at the next roundabout take 2nd exit. The drive now follows the foot of the Bathgate Hills and after ½ mile passes the turning to **Cairnpapple Hill Neolithic Sanctuary and Burial Cairn**. Further along this road are Beecraigs Country Park and the nearby AA viewpoint of Cockleroy Hill 913 feet (278 m).

The main tour proceeds through the village of **Torphichen**. The Preceptory (AM) was founded here in the 12th century as the headquarters of the Knights of St John of Jerusalem.

In a mile turn right on to the A706 (still signed Linlithgow) and 3½miles further turn right again with the A803 to enter **Linlithgow**. This former royal burgh, situated on Linlithgow Loch, is dominated by the splendid, but ruined, 15th- to 17-century Linlithgow Palace (AM) where Mary, Queen of Scots was born in 1542.

Follow Edinburgh signs and at the roundabout turn left. In 1½ miles cross the M9 and almost ½ mile further take the second main turning right on to the B903, signed Blackness. Later the shores of the Firth of Forth are reached at Blackness. Of interest here is the 15th-century **Blackness Castle** (AM).

From the castle return along the same road and in ¼ mile turn left on to the B9109, signed Edinburgh. A mile further turn left again on to the A904 (no sign) and pass the entrance to the **House of Binns** (NTS). This splendid building reflects the early 17th-century transition in Scottish architecture from the fortified stronghold to gracious mansion.

Continue along the A904 and in 2½ miles pass the turning to **Hopetoun House**. This magnificent mansion, is the home of the Marquis of Linlithgow and is considered to be the finest Scottish example of an Adam building.

Remain on the A904 for 1¾ miles then branch left with the B924, signed South Queensferry. Later pass beneath the Forth Road Bridge and enter **South Queensferry**. This pleasant small town retains several old houses and buildings including the Hawes Inn (1683). The **Forth Railway Bridge** was completed in 1890 and is one of the finest examples of engineering in the world.

In ½ mile pass beneath the railway bridge and 1 mile further pass the entrance to **Dalmeny House** *(on the left)*. This is the home of the Earl of Rosebery. It contains an important collection of furniture and paintings.

In ¾ mile join the main A90 and 2 miles further, at the Barnton Hotel, turn left on to an unclassified road, signed **Cramond**. A short detour is then made to visit the picturesque and historic village of Cramond.

Turn right into Cramond Road North and in just over ¼ mile turn left. After another ¾mile is the visitor's final place of interest — **Lauriston Castle**. Situated in pleasant gardens, this late 16th-century tower has been considerably extended and displays a fine collection of furniture and antiques.

In just over ¼ mile at the mini-roundabout go forward (no sign), then at the next T-junction turn left on to the A90 for the return to Edinburgh city centre.

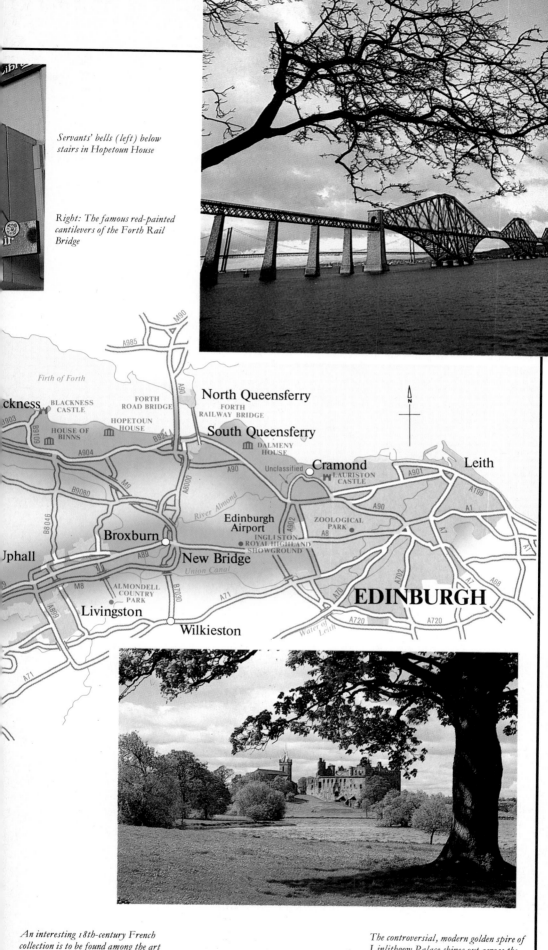

Servants' bells (left) below stairs in Hopetoun House

Right: The famous red-painted cantilevers of the Forth Rail Bridge

An interesting 18th-century French collection is to be found among the art treasures of Dalmeny House

The controversial, modern golden spire of Linlithgow Palace shines out across the loch

LEGEND

M8	Motorway
A71	Primary Route
A712	Main Road
B778	Secondary Road
8	Motorway Junction
122	Distance in miles to Edinburgh

EDINBURGH

MONTROSE 92
ARBROATH 79

NORTH BERWICK 24

BERWICK-UPON-TWEED 56

COLDSTREAM 49

JEDBURGH 48

ALNWICK 65

MORPETH 93

TYNEMOUTH 112

HEXHAM 96
CORBRIDGE 94
NEWCASTLE-UPON-TYNE 107
SUNDERLAND 119

CONSETT 105

ALSTON 122

DURHAM 129

HARTLEPOOL 138

BISHOP AUCKLAND 124

BROUGH 138

REDCAR 158
MIDDLESBROUGH 145
SALTBURN 159

DARLINGTON 147
STOCKTON ON TEES 144

WHITBY 177

SCOTCH CORNER 153

CHESTER 218 LONDON 405

Key to Places of Interest

1 Calton Hill	F6
2 Camera Obscura and Outlook Tower	D4
3 Canongate Church	F5
4 Canongate Tolbooth	F5
5 Childhood, Museum of	E4
6 City Art Centre	E4
7 City Chambers	E4
8 Colinton	B1
9 Commonwealth Pool, Royal	F1
10 Corstorphine	A3
11 Craigmillar Castle	F1
12 Cramond	A6
13 Dean Village	A5
14 Duddingston	F5
15 Edinburgh Castle	C4
16 Edinburgh Zoo	A3
17 George Heriot's School	D3
18 Georgian House, The	B5
19 Gladstone's Land	D4
20 Greyfriars Bobby	D3
21 Greyfriars Church	D3
22 Heart of Midlothian	D4
23 Hillend Ski Centre	B1
24 Holyrood Park & Arthur's Seat	F3
25 Huntly House	F4
26 John Knox House	E4
27 Lady Stair's House	D4
28 Lauriston Castle	A6
29 Leith	E6
30 Malleny Gardens	A3
31 Meadowbank Sports Centre	F6
32 The Meadows	D1
33 National Gallery of Scotland	D4
34 National Library of Scotland	D4
35 Palace of Holyrood House	F5
36 Parliament House	D4-E4
37 Portobello	F6
38 Princes Street & The Gardens	C4
39 Register House	E5
40 Royal Botanic Gardens	E6
41 Royal High School	F5
42 Royal Museum of Scotland (Chambers Street)	E3
43 Royal Museum of Scotland (Queen Street)	D6
44 Royal Observatory	F1
45 St Andrew's Church	D5
46 St Cuthbert's Church	B4
47 St Giles Church	E4
48 St Mary's Cathedral	A4
49 St Stephen's Church	C6
50 Scottish Agricultural Museum	A3
51 Scottish National Gallery of Modern Art	A5
52 Scott Monument	D5
53 Swanston	B1
54 Tron Church	E4
55 University of Edinburgh	E3
56 Usher Hall	B3
57 Water of Leith	A5
58 Wax Museum	E4
59 West Register House	B5
60 White Horse Close	F5

Street Index and Grid Reference

Central Edinburgh

Abercromby Place	C6-D6
Adam Street	F3
Ainslie Place	B5
Albany Street	D6-E6
Alva Street	A4-B4
Ann Street	A6
Argyle Place	D1
Athol Crescent	A3-A4-B4
Bank Street	D4
Belford Road	A5
Belgrave Crescent	A5
Bells Brae	A5
Bernard Terrace	F1
Blackfriars Street	E4
Bread Street	B3-C3
Bristo Place	D3-E3
Brougham Street	C2
Broughton Street	E6
Bruntsfield Place	B1-C1
Buccleuch Place	E2
Buccleuch Street	E2-F2-F1
Buckingham Terrace	A5-A6
Caledonian Crescent	A2
Caledonian Road	A2
Calton Road	E5-F5
Candlemaker Row	D3
Canning Street	A3-B3-B4
Canongate	E4-F4-F5
Castle Hill	D4
Castle Street	C5
Castle Terrace	B4-B3-C3
Chalmers Street	C2-D2
Chambers Street	D3-E3
Charlotte Square	B4-B5
Chapel Street	E2
Chester Street	A4
Clerk Street	F1-F2
Clyde Street	D6-E6
Coates Crescent	A4-B4
Cockburn Street	D4-E4
Comely Bank Avenue	A6
Cowgate	D4-E4-F4
Dalry Road	A3
Dean Bridge	A5
Dean Park Crescent	A6
Dean Terrace	B6
Dewar Place	A3-B3
Doune Terrace	B6
Drummond Street	E3-F3-F4
Drumsheugh Gardens	A4-A5
Dublin Street	D6
Dumbiedykes Road	F3-F4
Dundas Street	C6
Dundee Street	A1-A2
Earl Grey Street	B2-C2
East Cross Causeway	F2
East Market Street	E5-E4-F4-F5
East Preston Street	F1
Eton Terrace	A5-A6
Fingal Place	D1-E1
Forrest Road	D3
Fountain Bridge	A2-B2-B3-C3
Frederick Street	C5
Forth Street	E6
Gardener's Crescent	B2-B3
George IV Bridge	D3-D4
George Square	E2
George Street	B5-C5-D5
Gillespie Crescent	B1-C1
Gilmore Park	A1-A2
Gilmore Place	A1-B1-B2-C2
Gladstone Terrace	E1
Glengyle Terrace	C1
Gloucester Lane	B6
Grass Market	D3
Great King Street	C6
Greenside Row	E6-F6
Grindley Street	B3-C3
Grove Street	A2-A3
Hanover Street	C6-D6-D5
Hay Market	A3
Heriot Row	B6-C6
High Riggs	C2-C3
High Street	D4-E4
Hill Street	C5
Holyrood Road	F4
Home Street	C2
Hope Park Terrace	F1
Hope Street	B4
Howe Street	C6
India Place	B6
India Street	B6
Jeffrey Street	E4
Johnston Terrace	C3-C4-D4
Kier Street	C3-D3
King's Stables Road	B4-C4-C3
Lady Lawson Street	C3
Lauriston Gardens	C2
Lauriston Place	C2-C3-D3
Lauriston Street	C2-C3
Lawn Market	D4

Leamington Terrace	A1-B1
Leith Street	E5-E6
Lennox Street	A6
Leven Street	C1-C2
Leven Terrace	C1-C2
Livingstone Place	E1
Lochrin Place	B2-C2
London Road	F6
Lonsdale Terrace	C2
Lothian Road	B3-B4
Lower Gilmore Place	B1-B2
Lutton Place	F1
Manor Place	A4
Marchmont Crescent	D1
Marchmont Road	D1
Market Street	D4-E4
Melville Drive	C2-C1-D1-E1-F1
Melville Street	A4-B4-B5
Melville Terrace	E1-F1
Moray Place	B5-B6
Morrison Street	A3-B3
New Street	F4-F5
Nicolson Street	E3-E2-F2
Niddry Street	E4
North Bridge	E4-E5
North West Circus Place	B6
Northumberland Street	C6-D6
Oxford Terrace	A6
Palmerston Place	A3-A4
Panmure Place	C2
Picardy Place	E6
Pleasance	F3-F4
Ponton Street	B2-C2
Potter Row	E2-E3
Princes Street	B4-C4-C5-D5-E5
Queen Street	B5-C5-C6-D6
Queensferry Road	A5-A6
Queensferry Street	A5-B5-B4
Ramsey Lane	D4
Randolph Crescent	A5-B5
Rankeillor Street	F2
Regent Road	E5-F5
Regent Terrace	F5
Richmond Lane	F2-F3
Richmond Place	E3-F3
Rose Street	B5-C5-D5
Rothesay Place	A4-A5
Roxbury Place	F.3
Royal Circus	B6-C6
Royal Terrace	E6-F6
Rutland Square	B4
Rutland Street	B4
St Andrew Square	D5-D6
St Bernard's Crescent	A6-B6
St Giles Street	D4
St John Street	F4
St Leonards Hill	F2
St Leonards Lane	F2
St Leonard's Street	F1-F2
St Mary's Street	E4-F4
St Peter Place	A1
Sciennes	F1
Semples Street	B2-B3
Shandwick Place	B4
South Bridge	E3-E4
South Clerk Street	F1
South East Circus Place	C6
Spittal Street	C3
Stafford Street	A4-B4
Summerhall	F1
Sylvan Place	E1
The Mound	D4-D5
Tarvit Street	C2
Teviot Place	D3-E3
Thistle Street	C5-D5-D6
Torphichen Street	E3-E3
Upper Dean Terrace	B6
Upper Gilmore Place	B1
Victoria Street	D4
Viewforth	A1-B1
Viewforth Terrace	A1
Walker Street	A4-A5
Warrender Park Terrace	C1-D1
Waterloo Place	E5
Waverley Bridge	D4-D5
Wemyss Place	B5-B6
West Approach Road	A2-A3-B3
West Cross-Causeway	E2
West End	B4
West Maitland Street	A3-A4
West Port	C3
West Preston Street	F1
West Richmond Street	E3-F3
West Tollcross	B2
Whitehouse Loan	B1-C1
William Street	A4
York Place	D6-E6
Young Street	B5-C5

Key to Town Plan

AA Recommended roads	
Other roads	
Restricted roads	
Buildings of interest	College ▢
Churches	†
Car parks	�P
Parks and open spaces	▱
AA Service Centre	AA

Using the directory

The practical information in this Directory, including addresses, telephone numbers and opening times, is liable to change at short notice. While every effort has been made to ensure that it is comprehensive and up to date, the publishers cannot accept responsibility for errors or omissions, or for changes in the details given.

Telephone numbers

There is no need to dial 031 when telephoning within Edinburgh.

AA CLASSIFICATIONS

Hotels

★ Good hotels and inns, generally of small scale and with good furnishings and facilities.

★★ Hotels with a higher standard of accommodation. There should be 20% private bathrooms or showers.

★★★ Well-appointed hotels. Two-thirds of the bedrooms should have private bathrooms or showers.

★★★★ Exceptionally well-appointed hotels offering high standards of comfort and service. All bedrooms should have private bathrooms or showers.

★★★★★ Luxury hotels offering the highest international standards.

Restaurants

× Modest but good restaurant.

×× Restaurant offering a higher standard of comfort than above.

××× Well-appointed restaurant.

×××× Exceptionally well-appointed restaurant.

××××× Luxury restaurant.

Rosettes

The rosette award is used to highlight hotels and restaurants where it is judged that the food and service can be especially recommended.

❀ The food is of a higher standard than is expected for its classification.

❀❀ Excellent food and service, irrespective of its classification.

❀❀❀ Outstanding food and service, irrespective of its classification.

Camping and caravanning sites

► Site licence, 10% of pitches for touring units; site density not more than 30 per acre; 2 separate toilets for each sex per 30 pitches; good quality tapwater; efficient waste disposal; regular cleaning of ablutions block; fire precautions; well-drained ground.

►► All one-pennant facilities plus: 2 washbasins with hot and cold water for each sex per 30 pitches in separate washrooms; warden available at certain times of the day.

►►► All two-pennant facilities plus: one shower or bath for each sex per 30 pitches, with hot and cold water; electric shaver points and mirrors; all-night lighting of toilet blocks; deep sinks for washing clothes; facilities for buying milk, bread and gas; warden in attendance by day, on call by night.

►►►► All three-pennant facilities plus: a higher degree of organisation than one-three pennant sites; attention to landscaping; reception office; late-arrivals enclosure; first-aid hut; shop; routes to essential facilities lit after dark; play area; bad-weather shelter; hard standing for touring vans.

►►►►► A comprehensive range of services and equipment; careful landscaping; automatic laundry; public telephone; indoor play facilities for children; extra facilities for recreation; warden in attendance 24 hours per day.

Abbreviations

AM   Ancient Monuments in Scotland are the responsibility of the Scottish Development Department, 3–11 Melville St, Edinburgh EH3 7QD. Membership of the Friends of the Scottish Monuments can be purchased from the above address.

BH   Bank Holidays

ch 15 20p   children under 15 20p

ch 20p   children 20p

ER   Egon Ronay

Etr   Easter

ex   Except

Free   Admission free

NTS   National Trust for Scotland

Pen   Senior Citizens

PH   Public Holidays

For more details on the accommodation and eating out establishments listed, please see the current edition of the AA guides: *Hotels and Restaurants in Britain; Guesthouses, Farmhouses and Inns in Britain* and *Holiday Homes, Cottages and Apartments in Britain*, and the Egon Ronay Guides: *Healthy Eating Out; Pub Guide; Just a Bite* and *Egon Ronay's Guide to Hotels, Restaurants and Inns.*

How to get there

AIR SERVICES

Planes fly to and from Edinburgh from the following airports

London:

Gatwick	British Caledonian
Heathrow	British Airways, British Midland
Stansted	Air UK

Other UK airports:

Birmingham	British Airways
East Midlands	Air Ecosse
Glasgow	British Airways
Isle of Man	Manx Airlines
Manchester	Loganair, British Airways
Newquay	British Airways, Brymon Airlines
Norwich	Air UK
Plymouth	British Airways, Brymon Airlines
Wick (Highland)	Loganair, Air Ecosse

Channel Islands

Guernsey	Guernsey Airlines
Jersey	British Airways, Guernsey Airlines

Ireland:

Belfast	Loganair
Cork	British Airways, Aer Lingus

BRITISH RAIL

Frequent Inter City express trains run daily from **King's Cross Station** in London to Edinburgh, the journey takes approximately five hours.

An Inter City Motorail service operates from **Euston**, London to Edinburgh.

COACH SERVICES

National Express operate a network of express coach services throughout England and Wales and into Scotland from local coach and bus stations. Details are available from any National Express office or agent.

Cotter Coachline and Scottish City Link operate motorway express services from Victoria Coach Station in London. The journey time is approximately 8 hours.

Cotter Coachline
298 Regent Street, London W1 (no personal callers) 01-930 5781

Scottish City Link 298 Regent Street, London WIR 6LE
01-636 9373

BY ROAD

Edinburgh is approached from the south-east via the A1, A697 and A68; from the south-west via the M6, A74 and A702; from Glasgow via the M8 and A8; from Stirling via the M9 and A8; and from Perth and the north via the A9, M90 and the Forth Bridge.

Accommodation

HOTELS — The AA's choice

★ ★ ★ ★ ★ **Caledonian** Princes St (Pride of Britain) *031-225 2433* Telex no 72179

★ ★ ★ ★ **Carlton Highland** North Bridge (Scottish Highland) *031-556 7277* Telex no 727001

★ ★ ★ ★ **George** George St *031-225 1251* Telex no 72570

★ ★ ★ ★ **Ladbroke Dragonara** Bells Mill, 69 Belford Rd (Ladbroke) *031-332 2545* Telex no 727979

★ ★ ★ **Albany** 39–43 Albany St *031-556 0397* Telex no 727079

★ ★ ★ **Barnton Thistle** Queensferry Rd, (Thistle) *031-339 1144* Telex no 727928

★ ★ ★ **Braid Hills** 134 Braid Rd, Braid Hills (2½m S A702) *031-447 8888* Telex no 72311

★ ★ ★ **Bruntsfield** 69–74 Bruntsfield Pl (Best Western) *031-229 1393* Telex no 727897

★ ★ ★ **Crest** Queensferry Rd (Crest) *031-332 2442* Telex no 72541

★ ★ **Donmaree** 21 Mayfield Gdns *031-667 3641*

★ ★ ★ **Ellersly House** 4 Ellersly Rd (Embassy) *031-337 6888* Telex no 76357

★ ★ ★ **Howard** Great King St *031-557 3500* Telex no 727887

★ ★ ★ **King James Thistle** 107 St James Centre (Thistle) *031-556 0111* Telex no 727200

★ ★ ★ **Old Waverley** Princes St (Scottish Highland) *031-556 4648* Telex no 727050

★ ★ ★ **Post House** Corstorphine Rd (Trusthouse Forte) *031-334 8221* Telex no 727103

★ ★ ★ **Roxburghe** Charlotte Sq (Best Western) *031-225 3921* Telex no 727054

★ ★ ★ **Royal Scot** 111 Glasgow Rd (Swallow) *031-334 9191* Telex no 727197

★ ★ ★ **Stakis Commodore** West Marine Dr, Cramond Foreshore (Stakis) *031-336 1700* Telex no 727167

★ ★ ★ **Stakis Grosvenor** Grosvenor St (Stakis) *031-226 6001* Telex no 72445

★ ★ **Clarendon** Grosvenor St (Scottish Highland) *031-337 7033* Telex no 78215

★ ★ **Harp** St John's Rd, Corstorphine (3½m W on A8) (Osprey) *031-334 4750*

★ **Iona** Strathearn Pl *031-447 6264*

★ ★ **Murrayfield** 18 Corstorphine Rd (Alloa) *031-337 1844*

★ ★ **Suffolk Hall** 10 Craigmillar Pk *031-667 9328*

Capital (awaiting inspection) Clermiston Rd *031-334 3391*

OTHER RECOMMENDED HOTELS (ER)

Edinburgh Sheraton 1 Festival Sq *031-229 9131* Telex no 72398

GUESTHOUSES

Adam Hotel 19 Lansdowne Cres *031-337 1148*. Closed Xmas & New Year

Adria Hotel 11–12 Royal Ter *031-556 7875*. Closed Dec

Allison House 15/17 Mayfield Gdns *031-667 8049*. Closed Xmas & New Year

Ben Doran Hotel 11 Mayfield Gdns *031-667 8488*. Closed 20–27 Dec

Boisdale Hotel 9 Coates Gdns *031-337 1134*

Bonnington 202 Ferry Rd *031-554 7610*

Brunswick 7 Brunswick St *031-556 1238*

Buchan Hotel 3 Coates Gdns *031-337 1045*

Clans Hotel 4 Magdala Cres *031-337 6301*

Dorstan Private Hotel 7 Priestfield Rd *031-667 6721*. Closed 2 wks Xmas

Dunstane House 4 West Coates *031-337 6169*. Closed Xmas—4 Jan

Galloway 22 Dean Park Cres *031-332 3672* Telex no 72165

Glenisla Hotel 12 Lygon Rd *031-667 4098*

Greenside Hotel 9 Royal Ter *031-557 0022* Open Jan—Oct

Grosvenor 1 Grosvenor Gdns, Haymarket *031-337 4143*

Halcyon Hotel 8 Royal Ter *031-556 1033*. Closed Feb & New Year

Heriott Park 256 Ferry Rd *031-552 6628*

Hillview 92 Dalkeith Rd *031-667 1523*

Kariba 10 Granville Ter *031-229 3773*

Kildonan Lodge Hotel 27 Craigmillar Pk *031-667 2793*

Kingsley 30 Craigmillar Pk *031-667 8439*

Kirtle House 8 Minto St *031-667 2813*

Lindsay 108 Polwarth Ter *031-337 1580*

Marchall Hotel 14–16 Marchhall Cres *031-667 2743*

Marvin 46 Pilrig St *031-554 6605*

Newington 18 Newington Rd *031-667 3356*

Ravensdown 248 Ferry Rd *031-552 5438*

Rockville Hotel 2 Joppa Pans, Joppa (2m E off A1) *031-669 5418*

St Bernards 22 St Bernards Cres *031-332 2339*

St Margaret's 18 Craigmillar Pk *031-667 2202*

Salisbury Hotel 45 Salisbury Rd *031-667 1264*

Sherwood 42 Minto St *031-667 1200*. Closed Xmas & New Year

Southdown 20 Craigmillar Pk *031-667 2410*

Thrums Private Hotel 14 Minto St *031-667 5545*. Closed Xmas & New Year

Tiree 26 Craigmillar Pk *031-667 7477*

CAMPING AND CARAVANNING

▶▶▶▶**Mortonhall Caravan Park** (NT265680) 30 Frogston Rd East. Signposted. *031-664 1533* Open 28 Mar—Oct, booking advisable Jun—Aug

▶▶▶▶**Drum Mohr Caravan Park** (NT373734) Levenhall, Musselburgh. Signposted *031-665 6867* Open Mar—Oct, booking advisable Jul & Aug

▶▶▶**Little France Caravan Park** (NT289704) 219 Old Dalkeith Rd. Signposted *031-664 4742* Open Apr—Oct, booking advisable Jul & Aug

SELF-CATERING

Controller of Catering & Residences, **Heriot-Watt University** Riccarton, Currie, Edinburgh EH14 4AS. *031-449 5111 ext 2178* Self-contained flatlets, in three modern blocks on the University Campus, for 3–6 persons. 28 Jun–27 Sep

Keyplan Apartments Linton Court, Murieston Rd, Edinburgh EH11 2JJ. *031-337 4040* Forty-two units within a newly developed block of flats for 1–7 persons. Open all year
Vacation Accommodation (Box AA)

Pollock Halls of Residence 18 Holyrood Park Rd, Edinburgh EH16 5AY *031-667 1971* Student flats, within halls of residence, for 1–5 persons. Open 4 Jul–26 Sep

YOUTH HOSTELS

(*Not AA-appointed accommodation*) Low-priced accommodation for members of the Youth Hostels Association. Membership can be obtained from any hostel or from the Scottish Youth Hostels Association, address below:

Scottish Youth Hostels Association 161 Warrender Park Rd *031-229 8660*

Edinburgh Bruntsfield Youth Hostel 7 Bruntsfield Cres *031-447 2994*

Edinburgh Eglinton Youth Hostel 18 Eglinton Cres *031-337 1120*

YMCA Princes St *031-225 1174*

YWCA Randolph Pl *031-225 4379*

Eating and Drinking Out

(ER *indicates Egon Ronay–appointed
establishments*)

RESTAURANTS – The AA's choice

✗✗Alp-Horn 167 Rose St *031-225 4787*
Closed Sun, Mon, 2 wks from
Xmas Eve & 3 wks end June/
beginning Jul. Swiss cooking

✗✗L'Auberge 56 St Mary's St *031-556 58888*
French cooking

✗✗Champany Inn Town
2 Bridge Rd, Colinton *031-441 2587*
Steak restaurant

✗✗Lancers Brasserie 5 Hamilton
Pl, Stockbridge *031-332 3444*
North Indian & Bengali cooking

✗✗Lightbody's 23 Glasgow Rd *031-334 2300*
Closed Sun. British & French cooking

✗✗Martins 70–72 Rose St,
North Ln *031-225 3106*
Closed Sun, Mon, 26 Dec – 3 Jan
& 2 wks Jun/Jul. Lunch not
served Sat. Scottish, French &
Italian cooking

✗✗Ristorante Milano 7 Victoria
St *031-226 5260*
Closed Sun. Italian cooking

✗Chez Julie 110 Raeburn Pl *031-332 2827*
Closed Sun. French cooking

✗Kalpna 2–3 St Patrick Sq *031-667 9890*
Closed Sun. Indian vegetarian cooking

✗Kweilin Cantonese 19–21
Dundas St *031-557 1875*
Closed 25 Dec, 1 Jan & Chinese
New Year. Cantonese cooking

✗MacKintosh's 24A Stafford St *031-226 7530*
Closed Sun, 26, 27 Dec & 1, 2
Jan. Lunch not served Sat.
Scottish & French cooking

✗New Edinburgh Rendezvous
10A Queensferry St *031-225 2023*
Closed 25, 26 Dec, 1 Jan &
Chinese New Year. Chinese cooking

✗Shamiana 14 Brougham St *031-228 2265*
Closed 25 Dec & 1 Jan. Lunch
not served. Kashmiri & North
Indian cooking

✗Verandah Tandoori 17 Dalry
Rd *031-337 5828*
Bengali & North Indian cooking

OTHER RECOMMENDED RESTAURANTS (ER)

**Caledonian Hotel, Pompadour
Restaurant** Princes St *031-225 2433*
Closed 26 Dec & 2 Jan, lunch
not served Sat & Sun. French &
Scottish cooking

Donmaree Hotel Restaurant
21 Mayfield Gdns *031-667 3641*
Closed Sun & BH, lunch not
served Sat. French cooking

No 10 10 Melville Pl *031-225 8727*
Lunch not served Sun; dinner
not served Sun in winter.

LIGHT MEALS AND SNACKS (ER)

Brasserie Saint Jacques King
James Thistle Hotel, Leith St
031-556 0111
Closed 25 & 26 Dec

Handsel's Wine Bar 22 Stafford
St *031-225 5521*
Closed Sun, BH & 1 wk Jan

Helios Fountain 7 Grassmarket
031-229 7884
Closed Sun, 25, 26 Dec & 1, 2 Jan

Henderson's Salad Table
94 Hanover St *031-225 2131*
Closed Sun (except during
Festival) & BH

Laigh Kitchen 117a Hanover St
031-225 1552
Closed Sun & some BH

Sunflower Country Kitchen 4
South Charlotte St *031-220 1700*
Closed Sun, 25, 26 Dec & 1, 2 Jan

Waterfront Wine Bar 1c Dock Pl,
Leith *031-554 7427*
Closed Sun, 1, 2 Jan, 25 & 26 Dec

PUB FOOD (ER)

Cramond Inn Cramond Glebe Rd,
Cramond *031-336 2035*
Scottish & traditional bar food
served lunchtime only

Places to Visit

CITY CENTRE

Brass Rubbing Centre Canongate Tolbooth, 163 Canongate, Royal Mile 031-225 2424 ext 6638 Open Jun–Sep Mon–Sat 10–6; Oct–May Mon–Sat 10–5 Also open Sun during Edinburgh Festival 12 noon–5. Free (Charge for rubbing facilities)

Camera Obscura & Outlook Tower Visitor Centre Castle Hill 031-226 3709 Open daily Oct Mar 10–5; Apr–Sep 9.30–5.30 £1.45 (ch & pen 70p, students £1.10)

Candle Carvery and Museum Shop 140 High St 031-225 9566 Open daily 10–5.30. Free

Canongate Church Canongate The Royal Mile

Canongate Tolbooth 163 Canongate, Royal Mile 031-225 2424 ext 6638 Open Jun–Sep 10–6; Oct–May 10–5 Free

City Art Centre 2 Market St 031-225 2424 ext 6650 031-225 1131 after 5pm and weekends Open Mon–Sat 10–5 (10–6 Jun–Sep) & Sun 2–5 during Edinburgh Festival. Free

City Chambers High St 031-225 2424 Open when Council business permits weekdays 10–3. Free

Craigmillar Castle (AM) Craigmillar Open Apr–Sep Mon–Sat 9.30–7, Sun 2–7; Oct–Mar Mon–Sat 9.30–4, Sun 2–4 (closed Thu & Fri in winter) 50p (ch & pen 25p)

Edinburgh Castle (AM) Open 4 Jan–31 Mar & Oct–Dec Mon–Sat 9.30–4.20, Sun 12.30–3.35; Apr–Sep Mon–Sat 9.30–5.15, Sun 10.30–4.45. Castle closes 45 mins after the above times. £2 (ch & pen £1) Family £4.

Scottish National War Memorial Free. Also **Scottish United Services Museum** 031-225 7534 Open Mon–Sat 9.30–12.30 & 2–5, Sun 12.30–4.30. Free

Edinburgh Wax Museum 142 High St, Royal Mile 031-226 4445 Open daily 10–5 (last admission 4.30) £2.25 (ch 80p, pen 70p)

Edinburgh Zoo Corstorphine Rd

031-334 9171 Open all year Mon–Sat 9–6, Sun 9.30–6 (closes 5pm or dusk in winter) £2.50 (ch, pen & unemployed £1.25)

The Fruit Market Gallery 29 Market St 031-225 2383 Open Tue–Sat 10–5.30. Free

General Register House (East end of Princes St) 031-556 6585 Open all Year Mon–Fri 9–4.45 Closed certain PH. Free

George Heriot's School Lauriston Place 031-229 7263 Open Jul–Aug Mon–Fri 9.30–4.30, Sat 9.30–11. Free

Georgian House (NTS) 7 Charlotte Square 031-225 2160 Open Apr–Oct Mon–Sat 10–5, Sun 2–5; Nov, Sat 10–4.30, Sun 2–4.30 (last admission ½hr before closing) £1.50 (ch 75p) (includes audio-visual shows)

Gladstone's Land (NTS) 483 Lawnmarket High St 031-226 5856 Days and times of opening as Georgian House £1.50 (ch 75p)

Greyfriars Bobby Candlemaker Row

Greyfriars Tolbooth & Highland Kirk Kirk of the Greyfriars, George IV Bridge

Heart of Midlothian near the west door of St Giles Cathedral

Huntly House 142 Canongate 031-225 2424 ext 6689 031-225 1131 after 5pm and weekends) Open Mon–Sat, Jun–Sep 10–6; Oct–May 10–5 (Sun 2–5 during Edinburgh Festival). Free

John Knox House Museum 45 High St 031-556 6961 Open Mon–Sat 10–5; Nov–Mar 10–4 Last admission 4.30pm, winter 3pm £1 (ch & pen 70p)

Lady Stair's House off Lawnmarket 031-225 2424 ext 6593 (031-225 1131 after 5pm & weekends) Open Mon–Sat, Jun–Sep 10–6; Oct–May 10–5 (Sun 2–5 during Edinburgh Festival). Free

Lauriston Castle 2 Cramond Rd South, Davidson's Mains (on NW outskirts of Edinburgh, 1m E of Cramond) 031-336 2060 Open for guided tours only, Apr–Oct daily (ex Fri) 11–1 &

2–5 (last tour approx 4.20); Nov–Mar Sat & Sun only 2–4 (last tour approx 3.20) 80p (ch & pen 40p)

Magdalen Chapel Cowgate. For access contact Rev Sinclair Horne, Scottish Reformation Society, 17 George IV Bridge 031-225 1836

Museum of Childhood 42 High St (Royal Mile) 031-225 2424 ext 6646 Open Mon–Sat 10–6 (Oct–May 10–5) (Sun 2–5 during Edinburgh Festival). Free

National Gallery of Scotland The Mound 031-556 8921 Open Mon–Sat 10–5, Sun 2–5; winter lunchtime closure (Oct–Mar) 12–1 West Gallery, 1–2 East Gallery and New Wing (Mon–Sat 10–6, Sun 11–6 during Edinburgh Festival). Free

National Library of Scotland George IV Bridge 031-226 4531 Reading rooms open Mon–Fri 9.30–8.30, Sat 9.30–1. Exhibition Mon–Fri 9.30–5, Sat 9.30–1. Sun (Apr–Sep only) 2–5 Free Map Room Annexe 137 Causewayside Open Mon–Fri 9.30–5, Sat 9.30–1 Free

Nelson Monument Calton Hill Open Apr–Sep Mon 1–6, Tue–Sat 10–6; Oct–Mar Mon–Sat 10–3. 45p

New Town Conservation Centre 13a Dundas St 031-556 7054 Open Mon–Fri 9–1 & 2–5 Free

Old St Paul's Church Carruber's Close

Palace of Holyrood House (at E end of Canongate) 031-556 7371 Open Mon–Sat 9.30–3.45. Guided tour of State and Historic Apartments £1.50 (ch, pen & students 70p)

Parliament House with **Law Courts** Parliament Square (E of George IV Bridge) 031-225 2595 Open Mon–Fri 9.30–4 Free

Post Office Philatelic Bureau Waterloo Place 031-556 8661 Open Oct–Apr Mon–Fri 9–4.45, Sat 10–12.30; May–Sept Sat 10–12.30 Free

Royal Botanic Garden Inverleith Row 031-552 7171 ext 260 Garden open all year. Mar–Oct

Mon–Sat 9–1hr before sunset, Sun 11–1hr before sunset; Oct–Mar Mon–Sat 9–sunset, Sun 11–sunset. Plant houses & exhibition hall open Mon–Sat 10–5, Sun 11–5 (from 10am during Edinburgh Festival). Free

Royal Museum of Scotland Chambers St *031-225 7534*
Open Mon–Sat 10–5, Sun 2–5 Free

Royal Museum of Scotland 1 Queen St *031-225 7534*
Open Mon–Sat 10–5, Sun 2–5 Free

Royal Observatory Visitor Centre Blackford Hill *031-667 3321*
Open Mon–Fri 10–4, Sat & Sun 12–5. 65p (ch & pen 35p)

Royal Scottish Academy The Mound *031-225 6671*
Open Mon–Sat 10–5, Sun 2–5 £1.20 (ch & pen 50p)

St Giles' Cathedral High St

St Mary's Episcopal Cathedral Palmerston Place

St Mary's Roman Catholic Cathedral Broughton St

Scott Monument East Princes Street Gardens
Open Apr–Sep Mon–Sat 9–6; Oct–Mar Mon–Sat 9–3.45p

Scottish Craft Centre 140 Canongate, Royal Mile
Open Mon–Sat 10–5.30 Free

Scottish National Gallery of Modern Art Belford Rd *031-556 8921 ext 32*
Open all year Mon–Sat 10–5, Sun 2–5 (Mon–Sat 10–6, Sun 11–6 during Edinburgh Festival). Free

Scottish National Portrait Gallery 1 Queen St *031-556 8921*
Open Mon–Sat 10–5, Sun 2–5 (Mon–Sat 10–6, Sun 11–6 during Edinburgh Festival). Free

Talbot Rice Art Centre *031-667 1011 ext 4308*
Open all year Mon–Fri 10–5, Sat 10–1 Free

Tron Church Hunter Square

West Register House Charlotte Square *031-556 6585*
Open Mon–Fri, 9–4.45 (ex PH). Free

AROUND EDINBURGH

Aberdour Castle (AM)
Open Apr–Sep Mon–Sat 9.30–7, Sun 2–7; Oct–Mar Mon–Sat 9.30–4, Sun 2–4. Closed Thu am & Fri in winter. Admission fee payable

Andrew Carnegie Birthplace Museum, Moodie Street, Dunfermline *(0383) 724302*
Open all year daily. Apr–Oct Mon–Sat 11–5 (Wed 8pm), Sun 2–5; Nov–Mar 2–4 daily. Free

Blackness Castle (AM) 4½m NE of Linlithgow
Open Apr–Sep Mon–Sat 9.30–7, Sun 2–7; Oct–Mar Mon–Sat

9.30–4, Sun 2–4. Closed Mon pm & Tue in winter. Admission fee payable

Bo'ness and Kinneil Railway off Union St *(0506) 822298*
Trains run Etr, 6 May, 27 May & 26 Aug and weekends until end Sep

Bowhill, Selkirk (2½m off A708) *(0750) 20732*
Open Grounds May–Aug 12–5, riding centre all year. House & grounds 4 Jul–16 Aug Mon–Sat (closed Fri) 1–4.30, Sun 2–6 House & grounds £2, grounds only 80p

Castle Campbell (AM) and **Dollar Glen (NTS)**
Glen Open 4 Jan–23 Mar & 1 Oct–31 Dec Mon–Sat 9.30–4.20, Sun 12.30–3.35; 24 Mar–30 Sep Mon–Sat 9.30–5.05, Sun 11–5.05. Closed Thu pm & Fri in winter
Castle Open Apr–Sep Mon–Sat 9.30–7, Sun 2–7; Oct–Mar Mon–Sat 9.30–4, Sun 2–4. (Closed Thu pm & Fri in winter). Admission fee payable

Castle Jail Castlegate, Jedburgh *(0835) 63254*
Open Etr–mid Sep Mon–Sat 10–12 & 1–5, Sun 2–5.50p (ch 16, students, pen & unemployed 35p)

Crichton Castle (AM) Crichton
Open Apr–Sep Mon–Sat 9.30–7, Sun 2–7; Oct–Mar weekends only 2–4. Admission fee payable

Culross Abbey (AM) Culross
Open Apr–Sep Mon–Sat 9.30–7, Sun 2–7; Oct–Mar Mon–Sat 9.30–4, Sun 2–4. Free

Culross Palace (AM) Culross
Open Apr–Sep Mon–Sat 9.30–7, Sun 2–7; Oct–Mar Mon–Sat 9.30–4, Sun 2–4. Admission fee payable

Dalkeith Park Buccleuch Estate Dalkeith *031-663 5684*
Open end Mar–Oct daily 11–6, Nov wknds only 65p

Dalmeny House South Queensferry *031-331 1888*
Open 3 May–30 Sep, Sun–Thu 2–5.30 (last admission 5pm) £1.80 (ch 5–16 & students £1.20, pen £1.50)

Dawyck Botanic Garden on B712, 8m SW of Peebles *(07216) 254*
Open Apr–Sep daily 9–5.50p per car

Dirleton Castle (AM) Dirleton
Open Apr–Sep Mon–Sat 9.30–4, Sun 2–7 Oct–Mar Mon–Sat 9.30–4, Sun 2–4. £1 (ch & pen 50p)

Dryburgh Abbey (AM)
Open Apr–Sep Mon–Sat 9.30–7, Sun 2–7; Oct–Mar Mon–Sat 9.30–4, Sun 2–4. Admission fee payable

Dunfermline Abbey (AM) Pittencrieff Park, Dunfermline
Open Apr–Sep Mon–Sat 9.30–7, Sun 2–7; Oct–Mar Mon–Sat 9.30–4, Sun 2–4. Free

Earlshall Castle Leuchars *(033483) 205*
Open Etr- 27 Sep Thu–Sun 2–6 (last admission 5.15pm) £2 (ch 5–16 £1, pen £1.50)

Edinburgh Butterfly Farm Melville Nurseries, Lasswade *031-663 4932*
Open Apr–Oct daily 10–6, (10–5.30 Sat & Sun) £1.75 (ch & pen £1). Family Ticket, 2 adults and up to 4 children, £5

Edinburgh Crystal Visitors Centre, Eastfield, Penicuik (10 m S of Edinburgh) *(0968) 75128*
Open Mon–Sat 9–5, and some Sun Tours. Mon–Fri 9–3.30

Falkland Palace & Garden (NTS) Falkland *(0337) 57397*
Palace and Garden open Apr–Sep Mon–Sat 10–6, Sun 2–6; Oct Sat 10–6, Sun 2–6. Last visitors to Palace 5.15. Palace and Gardens £1.80 (ch 16 90p). Garden only £1.20 (ch 16 60p)

Fife Folk Museum The Weigh House, Ceres *(033482) 380* (curator's house)
Open Apr–Oct, Mon, Wed–Sat 2–5, Sun 2.30–5.30. Admission fee payable

Floors Castle Kelso *(0573) 23333*
Castle open Etr Sun & Mon, then 3 May–30 Sep Sun–Thu. Also open Fri in Jul & Aug 10.30–5.30 (last admission to Castle 4.45pm). Walled garden and garden centre, daily 9.30–5 £2 (ch 8 & over £1, pen £1.60). Grounds £1.20

Gladstone Court Museum, entrance by 113 High St, Biggar *(0899) 21050*
Open Etr–Oct daily 10–12.30, 2–5; Sun 2–5. Admission fee payable

Greenhill Covenanters House, Burn Braes, Biggar *(0899) 21050*
Open Etr–mid Oct daily 2–5, other times by arrangement. Admission fee payable

Hailes Castle (AM), East Linton (1m SW on unclassified rd)
Open Apr–Sep Mon–Sat 9.30–7, Sun 2–7; Oct–Mar Mon–Sat 9.30–4, Sun 2–4 (closed Wed pm and Thu in winter). Admission fee payable

Hill of Tarvit Mansion House & Garden (NTS), (2m S of Cupar off A916) *(0334) 53127*
Open Etr weekend, Apr & Oct Sat & Sun 2–6; May–Sep daily 2–6. Last admission ½hr before closing. Garden and grounds open all year 9.30–sunset. House & Garden–£1.80 (ch 90p). Garden only 60p (ch 30p)

The Hirsel, Coldstream (½m W on A697) *(0890) 2834*
Open during daylight hours. Admission by donation

Hopetoun House, South Queensferry (2m W on unclassified rd) *031-331 2451*
Open Etr then May–mid Sep daily 11–5 (last admission 5pm). Admission fee payable

House of the Binns (NTS) (4m E of Linlithgow off A904)
Open Etr then May–Sep daily (ex Fri) 2–5, last admission 4.30pm. Parkland daily 10–sunset £1.80 (ch 90p). Members of the Royal Scots Dragoon Guards free when in uniform

Jane Welsh Carlyle Museum, Lodge St Haddington *(062082) 3738*
Open Apr–Sep Wed–Sat 2–5 50p (accompanied ch free, pen 30p)

Jedburgh Abbey (AM)
Open Apr–Sep Mon–Sat 9.30–7, Sun 2–7; Oct–Mar Mon–Sat 9.30–4, Sun 2–4 Closed Thu pm & Fri in winter £1 (ch & pen 50p)

Kailzie Gardens
(2½m SE of Peebles on B7062) *(0721) 20007*
Open 4 Apr–11 Oct daily 11–5.30 £1 (ch 35p)

Kellie Castle & Gardens (NTS) (2m N of St Monans off B9171) *(03338) 271*
Castle open Etr & Oct Sat & Sun 2–6; May–Sep daily 2–6. Garden & grounds all year daily 10–sunset. Castle & gardens £1.80 (ch 90p). Gardens only 80p (accompanied ch 40p)

Kelso Abbey (AM)
Open Apr–Sep Mon–Sat 9.30–7, Sun 2–7; Oct–Mar Mon–Sat 9.30–4, Sun 2–4. Free

Kinneil House (AM), Bo'ness
Open Apr–Sep Mon–Sat 9.30–7, Sun 2–7; Oct–Mar Mon–Sat 9.30–4, Sun 2–4 (Closed Tue pm & Fri in winter) 50p (ch & pen 25p)

Linlithgow Palace (AM)
Linlithgow
Open Apr–Sep Mon–Sat 9.30–7, Sun 2–7; Oct–Mar Mon–Sat 9.30–4, Sun 2–4 £1 (ch & pen 50p)

Loch Leven Castle (AM), Castle Island, Kinross
Open Apr–Sep 9.30–7 (Sun 2–7) 50p (ch & pen 25p). Ferry charge

Malleny Garden (NTS), off Bavelaw Rd, Balerno
Open May–Sep daily 10–sunset £1 (ch 50p). Charge box

Manderston (1¼m E of Duns off A6105) *(0361) 83450*
Open 14 May–27 Sep, Sun & Thu 2–5.30. Also open BH. Admission fee payable

Mary, Queen of Scots House, Queen Street, Jedburgh *(0835) 63331*
Open Etr–Oct Mon–Sat 10–12 & 1–5, Sun 1–5 (& 10–12 Jun–Oct only) £1 (ch 16, unemployed, students & pen 75p)

Mellerstain House (3m S of Gordon on unclassified rd) *(057381) 225*
Open Etr, then May–Sep Mon–Fri & Sun 12.30–5. (Last admission 4.30pm). Admission fee payable

Melrose Abbey (AM), Melrose
Open Apr–Sep Mon–Sat 9.30–7, Sun 2–7; Oct–Mar Mon–Sat 9.30–4, Sun 2–4 £1 (ch & pen 50p)

Melrose Motor Museum, Newstead Rd, Melrose *(0835) 22356*
Open Apr–Oct, daily 10.30–5.30, Nov–Mar Sat & Sun 10–5. Admission fee payable

Museum of Flight, East Fortune Airport, East Fortune *031–225 7534*
Open Jul & Aug Mon–Sat 10–5, Sun 11–5, also Open days. Free

Myreton Motor Museum, Aberlady *(08757) 288*
Open daily 10–6 (10–5 in winter) £1 (ch 16 25p)

Neidpath Castle, Peebles *(08757) 201*
Open 16 Apr–Oct, Mon–Sat 10–1 & 2–6, Sun 1–6, subject to the availability of staff. 75p (ch 14 20p, ch under 4 free, pen 50p)

Nether Mill (Peter Anderson Ltd), Huddersfield St, Galashiels *(0896) 2091*
Open Apr–Nov Mon–Sat 9–5, (Jun–Sep Sun 12–5); Mill tours Mon–Fri between 10.30–2. Free

Pinkie House, Musselburgh *031–665 2059*
Open mid Apr–mid Jul & mid Sep–mid Dec, Tue 2–5. Free

Preston Mill (NTS), East Linton *(0620) 860426*
Open Apr–Sep Mon–Sat 10–12.30 & 2–5.30, Sun 2–5.30; Oct Mon–Sat 10–12.30 & 2–4.30, Sun 2–4.30; Nov–Mar Sat 10–12.30 & 2–4.30, Sun 2–4.30 £1 (ch 16 50p)

Priorwood Garden (NTS), Melrose *(089682) 2965*
Open Apr & 1 Nov–24 Dec, Mon–Sat 10–1 & 2–5.30; May–Jun & Oct Mon–Sat 10–5.30, Sun 1.30–5.30; Jul–Sep Mon–Sat 10–6, Sun 1.30–5.30. Donations

St Andrews Castle (AM), St Andrews
Open Apr–Sep Mon–Sat 9.30–7, Sun 2–7; Oct–Mar Mon–Sat 9.30–4, Sun 2–4. Admission fee payable

St Andrews Cathedral & Museum (AM), St Andrews
Open Apr–Sep Mon–Sat 9.30–7, Sun 2–7; Oct–Mar Mon–Sat 9.30–4, Sun 2–4.50p (ch 25p)

Scottish Agricultural Museum, Royal Highland Showground, Ingliston *031–225 7534*
Open May–Sep Mon–Fri 10–5, Sun 11–5. Free

Scottish Fisheries Museum, St Ayles, Harbour Head, Anstruther *(0333) 310628*
Open Nov–Mar daily (ex Tue) 2–5; Apr–Oct Mon–Sat 10–5.30, Sun 2–5 £1 (ch 16, pen & unemployed 50p)

Scottish Mining Museum, Lady Victoria Colliery, Newtongrange *031–663 7519*
Open Tue–Fri 10–4.30, Sat & Sun 12–5. Admission fee payable

Scottish Museum of Woollen Textiles, Tweedvale Mill, Walkerburn *(089687) 281 & 283*
Open Etr–Oct Mon–Sat 10–5, Sun 12–4.30 winter Mon–Fri 10–5. Admission fee payable

Smailholm Tower (AM) (1½m SW of Smailholm)
Open Apr–Sep Mon–Sat 9.30–7, Sun 2–7; Oct–Mar Mon–Sat 9.30–4, Sun 2–4.50p (ch 25p)

Tantallon Castle (AM) (2m E of North Berwick on A198)
Open Apr–Sep Mon–Sat 9.30–7, Sun 2–7; Oct–Mar Mon–Sat 9.30–4, Sun 2–4. (Closed Tue & alternate Wed in winter) £1 (ch & pen 50p)

Thirlestane Castle & Border Country Life Museum, Lauder *(05782) 254*
Open Etr, May, Jun & Sep, Wed, Thu & Sun; Jul & Aug daily ex Sat. Castle & Museum 2–5; Grounds 12–6. £2 (ch & pen £1.50). Family £5

Torphichen Preceptory (AM)
Open Apr–Sep Mon–Sat 9.30–7, Sun 2–7; Oct–Mar Mon–Sat 9.30–4, Sun 2–4, closed Fri & alternate Wed.
Closed in winter 50p (ch & pen 25p)

Town House & The Study (NTS), Culross *(0383) 880359*
Open: House Etr & May–Sep Mon–Fri 10–1 & 2–5, Sat & Sun 2–5; Study Apr–Oct Sat & Sun 2–4 also by appointment. House 50p (ch & pen 25p). Study 30p (ch & pen 15p)

Traquair House, Traquair (1m S of Innerleithen on B709) *(0896) 830323*
Open 12 Apr–18 Oct 1.30–5.30. Jul, Aug & first 2 weeks in Sep open 10.30–5.30. Last admission 5pm. Admission fee payable

Tyninghame Gardens, Dunbar (1m N of A1 between Dunbar & East Linton) *(0620) 860330*
Open Jun–Sep Mon–Fri 10.30–4.30. Admission fee payable

Entertainment

THEATRES AND CONCERT HALLS

Assembly Rooms, 54 George St, *031-226 5992*
  International lunchtime concerts
Church Hill Theatre, Morningside Rd *031-447 7597*
King's Theatre, Leven St *031-229 1201*
  Scottish Opera, musicals, pantomimes
The Netherbow Arts Centre, 43 High St *031-556 9579*
The Playhouse Theatre, 22 Greenside Pl *031-557 2590*
  Scottish Ballet; rock concerts; grand opera
The Queen's Hall, Clerk St *031-668 3456*
  Home of the Scottish Chamber Orchestra and the Scottish Baroque Ensemble; also jazz and pop concerts, folk music, recitals and lectures
Royal Lyceum Theatre, Grindlay St *031-229 9697*
The Scottish Youth Theatre, 48 Albany St *031-557 0962*
Theatre Workshop, 34 Hamilton Place *031-226 5425*
Traverse Theatre, 112 West Bow, Grassmarket *031-226 2633*
  New work by contemporary Scottish and international writers
Usher Hall, Lothian Rd *031-228 1155*
  Scottish Chamber Orchestra; Scottish National Orchestra

CINEMAS

Cameo Cinema, Tollcross *031-228 4141*
Cannon 1, 2 & 3, 120 Lothian Rd *031-229 3030*
Classic Cinema, 50 Nicolson St

031-667 1839
Dominion Cinemas, Newbattle Terrace *031-447 2660*
Filmhouse, 88 Lothian Rd *031-228 2688*
Odeon Theatre, Clerk St *031-667 7331/2*

DISCOS/NIGHTCLUBS

Amphitheatre, Lothian Rd *031-229 7670*
  Most modern lightshow in Scotland
Buster Browns, 25 Market St *031-226 4224*
  Open Thu – Sun 9.30pm – 3am
Cinderellas Rockerfellers, St Stephen St *031-556 0266*
  Open Tue – Sun
Coasters Discotheque Complex, 3 West Tollcross *031-228 3252*
  Open Fri – Sun
Dillingers, 28 King's Stables Rd *031-228 3547*
  Open Thu – Sun
Madhatters, 126 High St *031-225 4343*
  Open Fri 9pm – 3am; Sat 10pm – 3am
Madisons, Greenside Place (next to Playhouse) *031-557 3807*
  Open Thu, Fri & Sat (Sun from March onwards), 21 + 9.30pm – 3am
Top 'O' Nightspot, 40 Grindlay St *031-229 6697*
  Open daily 10pm – 3am
Zenatec, 3 Semple St *031-229 7733* (night), *031-229 8522* (day)
  Open Fri, Sat & Sun

CASINOS

The Berkeley Casino Club, 2 Rutland Place *031-228 4446*
  Open Mon – Fri 2pm – 4am, Sat 2pm – 2am, Sun 7.30pm – 4am (membership takes 48hrs to

process)
Casino Martell, 7 Newington Rd *031-667 7763*
  Open Mon – Fri 10pm – 4am; Sat 10pm – 2am; Sun 10pm – 4am
Royal Chimes Casino, 3 Royal Terrace *031-556 1055*
  Mon – Fri 2pm – 4am; Sat 7pm – 2am; Sun 9pm – 4am
Stakis Regency Casino, 14 Picardy Place *031-557 3585*
  Mon – Fri 2pm – 4am; Sat 2pm – 2am; Sun 7.30pm – 4am (membership takes 48hrs to process)

EVENING/LUNCHTIME ENTERTAINMENT

Bannermans Bar, 212 Cowgate *031-556 3254*
  Jazz, blues, folk
Platform One, Caledonian Hotel, Rutland St *031-225 2433*
  Folk, blues, jazz
Crest Hotel, Queensferry Rd *031-332 2442*
  Jazz

SCOTTISH EVENINGS

The hotels listed below offer an evening of traditional Scottish food and entertainment.

George Hotel, George St *031-225 1251*
King James Thistle Hotel, Leith St *031-556 0111*
Learmonth Hotel, 18 – 20 Learmonth Terrace *031-343 2671*
  Entertainment only
North British Hotel, Princes St *031-556 2414*
Round Stables, Prestonfield House Hotel, Prestonfield Rd, Prestonfield *031-668 3346*

Recreation and Sports

BOWLING GREENS

Balgreen
Canaan Grove
St Margarets Park, Corstorphine
Dalmeny Street
Harrison
Inverleith Park
Jessfield
Leith Links
Loaning Crescent
The Meadows (East and West)
Montgomery Street
Oxgangs
Powderhall
Prestonfield
Stenhouse
Victoria Park

FISHING

RESERVOIRS AND LOCHS
These are located near Edinburgh and are mainly stocked with brown and/or rainbow trout.
Bonaly Reservoir (no permit required)
Clubbiedean Reservoir
Crosswood Reservoir
Gladhouse Reservoir
Glencourse Reservoir
Harlaw Reservoir
Harperrig Reservoir
  Permits for the above are available from Lothian Regional Council, Department of Water and Drainage, *031-445 4141*
Donolly Reservoir
Hopes Reservoir
  Permits available from Lothian

Regional Council, Department of Water and Drainage, Alderston House, Haddington *(062 082) 4131*
Duddingston Loch (carp, perch, roach, tench). Permits available from Scottish Development Dept, 3 – 11 Melville St, Edinburgh. *031-226 2570*

RIVERS
River Esk Permits from T Mealyou, Sports Shop, 11 Newbiggin, Musselburgh
River Esk (North) Permits from Esk Valley Angling Improvement Association, Kevin Burns, 53 Fernieside Crescent, Edinburgh *031-664 4685*. Local shops. Officials on river

Water of Leith Permits from Lothian Regional Council Reception, George IV Bridge, Edinburgh

River Tyne Permits from J S Main (Saddlers), 87 High St, Haddington

Union Canal Permits from Lothian Regional Council. Ranger, Union Canal

SEA AND SHORE

There is sea and shore angling at South Queensferry and Musselburgh. In Edinburgh there is shore angling at Cramond, the mouth of the River Almond, and from Seafield to Portobello.

FOOTBALL

Heart of Midlothian Football Club, Tynecastle Park *031-337 6132*

Hibernian Football Club, Easter Road Park *031-661 2159*

GOLF COURSES

Visitors are generally welcome at the golf clubs listed below. Some clubs do impose certain restrictions and where this is the case these have been noted at the end of each entry. It is advisable to telephone in advance and check when starting times are available. Clubs and trolleys are available for hire at many clubs. For more details on golf courses, please see the current edition of *AA Guide to Golf Courses in Britain.*

NEAR CITY CENTRE *(within 5-mile radius)*

Braid Hills Golf Courses (2 municipal courses) Braid Hills Approach *031-447 6666* 2½ miles from the city centre off the A702

The Bruntsfield Links Golfing Society Ltd 32 Barnton Ave *031-336 1479* 4 miles north-west of the city off the A90 to Queensferry. Members of recognised golf clubs require a letter of introduction

Carrick Knowe Golf Course (municipal course) off Balgreen Rd *031-337 1096* 2 miles west of the city centre, off the A8.

Craigentinny Golf Course (municipal course) Craigentinny Ave *031-554 7501* 2½ miles east of the city centre off A199 Seafield Road

Craigmillar Park Golf Club 1 Observatory Rd *031-667 0047* 2½ miles south of city centre off A701. Terms for visitors available from the Secretary

Duddingston Golf Club Duddingston Rd West *031-661 7688* (Secretary) 3 miles east of the city centre on the A1

Gogarburn Hospital Golf Club Gogarburn Hospital *031-339 4242*

Off the main Edinburgh/Glasgow road, west of the Maybury roundabout

Kingsknowe Golf Club 326 Lanark Rd *031-441 1145* 3 miles south-west from city centre on A70 Restrictions on visitors at weekends

Liberton Golf Club Kingston Grange, 297 Gilmerton Rd *031-664 3009* 2½ miles south-east of the city centre off the A68

Lothianburn Golf Club Biggar Rd *031-445 2288* 5 miles south of the city centre on the A702. Restricted times for visitors at weekends

Mortonhall Golf Club 231 Braid Rd *031-447 2411* 4 miles south of city centre, on Braid Road off A702. Visitors require a letter of introduction from their home club

Murrayfield Golf Club 43 Murrayfield Rd *031-337 3478* 2 miles west of city centre off the A8. Visitors require a letter of introduction from their home club and must book in advance by telephone. Weekdays only.

Portobello Golf Course (municipal course) Stanley St *031-669 4361* 3 miles east of the city centre off the A1

Prestonfield Golf Club Prestonfield Rd North *031-667 1273* 1½ miles south-east of city centre off the A68. Members of recognised golf clubs welcome. Some weekend restrictions

Ravelston Golf Club 24 Ravelston Dykes Rd *031-332 3486* 2½ miles west of city centre between the A90 and the A8 Visitors (from outside Scotland) welcome weekdays

The Royal Burgess Golfing Society Whitehouse Rd, Barton *031-339 2075* (Secretary) 4 miles north-west of city centre off the A90. Visitors welcome weekdays on application to the Secretary

Silverknowes Golf Course (municipal) Silverknowes Parkway *031-336 3843* 4 miles north-west of the city centre off the A90

Swanston Golf Club Swanston Rd *031-445 2239* 5 miles south of city centre off A702

Torphin Hill Golf Club Torphin Rd, Colinton *031-441 1100* 3 miles south-west of city centre off A720

Turnhouse Golf Club 154 Turnhouse Rd, Corstorphine *031-339 7701* 5 miles west of city, near Edinburgh Airport

Port Royal Golf Range Eastfield Rd (next to Edinburgh Airport) *031-335 4377* Open daily. Floodlit bays;

practice sand bunkers; putting green; professional tuition

FURTHER AFIELD

Blairgowrie Golf Club Rosemount, Blairgowrie *(0250) 2622* 1½ miles south of Blairgowrie on the A93. Starting times to be booked in advance in writing. Some restrictions Wednesdays and weekends

Dalmahoy Country Club Kirknewton *031-333 1845* 7½ miles west of Edinburgh on the A71

Gleneagles Hotel Golf Courses Auchterarder *(07646) 3543* 2 miles west of Auchterarder on A823

Gullane Golf Club Gullane *(0620) 843115* 21 miles north-east of Edinburgh on the A198. Some restrictions on No 1 course

The Honourable Company of Edinburgh Golfers Muirfield, Gullane *(0620) 842123* 18 miles east of Edinburgh on the A198. Visitors must make prior application through home golf club secretary

Ladybank Golf Club Ladybank *(0337) 30320* 6 miles south of Cupar

The Links Golf Course Musselburgh. On the A1 next to Musselburgh Racecourse

Longniddry Golf Club Longniddry *(0875) 52141* 13 miles east of Edinburgh. No visitors Fridays and weekends

Lundin Golf Club Golf Rd, Lundin Links *(0333) 320202* 13 miles east of Kirkcaldy on A915

The Musselburgh Golf Club Monktonhall, Musselburgh *031-665 2005* East of Edinburgh off the A1. Visitors must book in advance in writing

North Berwick Golf Club The Clubhouse, West Links, North Berwick *(0620) 2666* North-east of Edinburgh off the A198

Ratho Park Golf Club Ratho, Newbridge *031-333 1752* 8 miles west of Edinburgh

Royal Musselburgh Golf Club Prestongrange House, Prestonpans *(0875) 276* 9 miles east of Edinburgh on the A198

St Andrews Links Management Committee, Golf Place, St Andrews (4 public courses) *(0334) 75757* for advance bookings

GREYHOUND RACING

Powderhall Stadium Beaverhall Rd *031-556 8141* (Also athletics)

HORSE RACING

Musselburgh Racecourse *031-665 2859*

ICE SPORTS

Murrayfield Ice Rink Riversdale
Crescent *031-337 6933*
Skating, ice hockey, curling

MOTOR RACING

Royal Highland Showground
Ingliston. A road racing circuit,
meetings are held from April to
October

PONY TREKKING AND RIDING

Grange Riding Centre Mrs E
Knight, West Calder
(0506) 871219
Silverknowes Riding Centre
Muirhouse Parkway *031-332 5750*
Tower Farm Riding Stables Mrs
J Forrest, 85 Liberton Drive *031-664 3375*

PUTTING

Bruntsfield
St Margarets Park, Corstorphine
Harrison
Inverleith
Leith Links
Pilrig Park
Portobello (Novelty golf)
East Princes Street Gardens
Rosefield
Saughton
Victoria Park

PITCH AND PUTT

Bruntsfield Park
18 holes
Inverleith Park
Apr – Sep, 9 holes

RUGBY

**Murrayfield Scottish Rugby
Union Ground** Roseburn St
031-337 8993

SKIING

Hillend Ski Centre Biggar Rd
Pentland Hills *031-445 4433*
400-metre artificial ski slope

SNOOKER

Angle Club 3 Jordan Lane *031-447 8700*
**Cuemasters Snooker and Social
Club** 183 Constitution St *031-554 0971*
Davis Snooker Club
24 Annandale St *031-557 4579*
Marco's Leisure Centre 51 – 95
Grove Street *031-228 2141*
Snooker and Squash Centre
146 Slateford Rd *031-443 2211*

SPORTS CENTRES

Craiglockhart Sports Centre
177 Colinton Rd *031-443 0101/2*
Jack Kane Centre 208 Niddrie
Main Rd *031-669 0404*

Meadowbank Sports Centre
139 London Rd *031-661 5351*
Saughton Sports Centre *031-443 0101/2*

SWIMMING

Telephone enquiries for all the
swimming centres listed below
should be directed to the Royal
Commonwealth Pool *031-667 7211*

Dalry Teaching Centre
Caledonian Crescent
Open Mon – Fri, 12 noon – 1.20;
Tue, Thu & Fri 5.30 – 8; Sat
9 – 4; Sun 9 – 12noon
Glenogle Swimming Centre
Glenogle Rd
Open Mon – Fri 12noon – 8; Sat
9 – 4; Sun 9 – 12noon
**Infirmary Street Swimming
Centre** Infirmary St
Open Mon – Fri 8 – 8; Sat 9 – 4
Leith Swimming Centre
Junction Pl, Leith
Open Mon – Fri 9 – 8; Sat 9 – 4
Portobello Swimming Centre
Bellfield St
Open Mon – Fri 9 – 8; Sat 9 – 6
Royal Commonwealth Pool 21
Dalkeith Rd
Open Mon – Fri 9 – 9; Sat & Sun
10 – 4 (swimming, diving, sauna/
solarium suite, fitness centre,
rowing tank, pool tables etc)

Shopping

There are pedestrian shopping
precincts at Rose Street (between
Princes Street and George Street),
in the St James' Centre and the
Waverley Market. Most of the
larger shops and department stores
(British Home Stores, C & A,
Frasers, Jenners, Littlewoods,
Marks & Spencer) are situated in
Princes Street.

ANTIQUE SHOPS

Alexander Adamson, 48 St
Stephen St *031-225 7310*
General antiques, Georgian
furniture, porcelain, glass
Aldric Young, 49 Thistle St *031-226 4101*
Late 18th- and early 19th-
century antiques
Joseph Bonnar, 72 Thistle St *031-226 2811*
Antique and period jewellery,
small silver
Carson Clark Gallery, (Scotia
Maps) 173 Canongate *031-556 4710*
Antique maps
Castle Antiques, 330 Lawnmarket
031-225 7615
Furniture, china, pictures, silver
**Cavanagh (The Collector's
Shop),** 49 Cockburn St *031-226 3391*
Coins, medals, postcards,
antique silver, militaria

Court Curio Shop,
519 Lawnmarket *031-225 3972*
Jewellery, general
Paul Couts, 101 West Bow *031-225 3238*
18th-century furniture
Eric Davidson, 4 Grassmarket
031-225 5815
Furniture, porcelain, silverware,
paintings
Dunedin Antiques, 4 North West
Circus Pl *031-226 3074*
Furniture, metalwork
Tom Fidelo, 49 Cumberland St
031-557 2444
Antique paintings
Fifteen Grassmarket, 15
Grassmarket *031-226 3087*
Period clothes. Open Mon – Fri
1 – 7pm, all day Sat
Fyfes Antiques, 41 & 48 Thistle
St *031-225 4287*
Furniture, porcelain, oil
paintings
Goodwin, 15 Queensferry St *031-225 4717*
Silver jewellery
Herrald, 38 Queen St *031-225 5939*
Antique furniture, silver, brass
Humphrey, 38 Victoria St *031-226 3625*
Postcards, china, glass, paintings
Letham Antiques, 20 Dundas St
031-556 6565
Furniture, silver, jewellery,
decorative items. Closed Mon

Linton, 95 West Bow *031-226 6946*
Prints, paintings, bric-a-brac
John McIntosh, 60 Grassmarket
031-225 1165
Fine art, porcelain, bric-a-brac
Penny Farthing, 7 Beaufort Rd
031-447 2410
General
West Bow Antiques, 102 West
Bow *031-226 2852*
John Whyte, 116 Rose St *031-226 2377*
Jewellery, silver (new and
antique)
Whytock and Reid, Sunbury
House, Belford Mews *031-226 4911*
18th- and 19th-century British
furniture, oriental carpets and
rugs, church furnishings
Wildman Brothers, 54 Hanover
St *031-225 6754*
Jewellery, china, silver

BOOKSHOPS

Automobile Association, 18 – 22
Melville St
Bauermeister Booksellers,
19 George IV Bridge
Edinburgh Bookshop, 57 George
St
Church of Scotland Bookshop,
117 George St
James Thin, 53 South Bridge
Waterstone's Booksellers,
114 George St.

CRAFT SHOPS

Curio Imports, 14 & 44 Leven St
031-229 0899
Oriental curios and crafts,
oriental clothes

Ian Clarkson, 87 West Bow *031-225 8141*
Contemporary British craft
jewellery

Eastern Crafts, 251/253
Canongate *031-556 6553*
Oriental curios and crafts

Edinburgh Candles Shop, 42
Candlemaker Row *031-225 9646*
Candles, cards, incense

Innes Art, 219 Bruntsfield Pl *031-447 8929*
Art, jewellery

Langue de Chat, Unit 8, Waverley
Market *031-556 8100*
Designer knitwear

Potters Choice, 13 St Mary's St
031-556 6751
Pottery, crafts, giftwrap

Romulus, 136 Rose St *031-226 5269*
Glass, soft toys, pottery, gifts

Royal Mile Miniatures,
154 Canongate *031-557 2293*
Specialises in making furniture
for dolls' houses

Sandpiper Crafts, 106 Rose St *031-226 6211*
Jewellery, gifts, giftwrap, crafts

Clare Schilska, 46 Candlemaker
Row *031-225 1191*

Scotrocks, 10 Grassmarket *031-226 6383*

Scottish Craft Centre,
140 Canongate *031-556 6051*
Display of selected Scottish craft
work for sale. Exhibitions,
advisory service.
Open Mon–Sat 10–5.30,
admission free

Studio One, 10–14 Stafford St
031-226 5812
Also furniture shop at 132
Morningside Rd and kitchen
shop at 71 Morningside Rd

Anne Thomas Fabrics,
274 Canongate *031-557 1503*

DELICATESSENS

The Good Food Shop, 213 St
John's Rd *031-334 2159*

Henderson's, 94 Hanover St *031-225 2131*
Vegetarian, wholefood

Herby's Delicatessen,
66 Raeburn Pl *031-332 9888*

**Nastiuk Continental
Delicatessen** 10 Gillespie Pl *031-229 7054*
International food specialist

Newington Road Delicatessen,
84 Newington Rd *031-667 2969*
Wholefood, continental
specialities, duck, quail, goose

Valvona & Crolla, 19 Elm Row
031-556 6066
Continental food and wine

Victor Hugo Delicatessen,
26–27 Melville Terr *031-667 1827*
Continental meats, paté,
farmhouse cheese, fish

DRY CLEANER

Pullars, 23 Frederick St *031-225 8095*
Mon–Fri 8.30–5.30 Sat 8.30–1

TARTANS AND WOOLLENS

Discount Highland Supply,
7 Cowgatehead

Edinburgh Woollen Mill,
62 & 139 Princes St

**Geoffrey (Tailor) Highland
Crafts,** 57–59 High St

Gleneagles of Scotland, 371 High
St

The House of Macpherson,
17 West Maitland St, Haymarket

The Kilt Shop, 21–25 George IV
Bridge

Kinloch Anderson Ltd, John
Knox House, 45 High St

Pitlochry Knitwear, 28 North
Bridge

Rodger of the Royal Mile,
3 Canongate

The Scotch House, 60 Princes St

Romanes & Paterson, 62 Princes
St

Scotia Kilt Shop,
84 Causewayside

Tartan Gift Shop, 96–96a Princes
St

Transport

BUS SERVICES

For local bus and tour information
contact:

Lothian Region Transport 5
Waverley Bridge *031-226 5087*
and *031-554 4494* (lost property)

Eastern Scottish Buses St
Andrew Square Bus Station *031-556 8464*

Last buses to termini leave the city
centre Mon–Sat at 11.30pm, Sun
11pm (times approx). There are
five circular night bus services
from Waverley Bridge which serve
many parts of the city and
immediate areas, Mon–Fri 0.15am,
1.15am, 2.15am, 3.15am and
4.15am; Sat & Sun 0.15am, 1.15am
2.15am and 3.15am.

A Freedom Ticket, available
from Lothian Region Transport
and the Tourist Information Centre
allows unlimited use of the city
buses for one day (not valid for the
Airport Service).

An Airport Bus, service 100,
operates between Edinburgh
Airport and Waverley Bridge.
Timetables are available from
Lothian Region Transport, address
as above.

CAR HIRE

When making enquiries, ask for a
fully inclusive rate to include car
hire, insurance, 15% VAT, any
mileage charge and any other
surcharges. Also check your
liability in case of any damage to
the vehicle as you may have to pay
the first part of a claim even if you
have paid insurance.

Arnold Clark Lochrin, Tolcross
031-229 8911

Avis Rent A Car 100 Dalry Rd
031-337 6363

Avis Rent A Car Terminal
Building, Edinburgh Airport
031-333 1866

Bradbury Vehicle Rentals 37–40
Haddington Pl *031-556 1406*

Budget Rent A Car 116 Polwarth
Gardens *031-228 6088*

City Car Rental Coach Terminal,
14 Lothian Rd *031-228 3409*

Edinburgh Car and Van Rental
9 Cranston St *031-556 1666*

Forth Car Hire Learmonth Hotel
19 Learmonth Terr *031-343 1001*

Godfrey Davis Europcar 24 East
London St *031-661 1252*

Godfrey Davis Europcar
Terminal Building, Edinburgh
Airport *031-333 2588*

Godfrey Davis Europcar
Waverley Rail Drive Kiosk *031-556 8835*

Hertz Rent A Car 10 Picardy Pl
031-556 8311

Mitchells Self Drive
32 Torphichen St *031-229 5384*

Roadrunner Car Hire
24 Haymarket Terr *031-337 1319*

Total Car Rental 45 Lochrin Pl
031-229 4548

Wards Car Rentals 16 Annandale
St *031-557 0304*

Wheels Auto Rent 36 Canaan Ln,
Morningside *031-447 6184*

CAR PARKS

MULTI-STOREY CAR PARKS
St James Centre, Castle Terrace

SURFACE CAR PARKS
Crichton Street
Haymarket Terrace
Holyrood Road
Lauriston Place
Leith Street
Morrison Street
St Leonard's Street
West Nicolson Street

TAXIS

Castle Cars 2 Torphichen St *031-228 2555*

Central Radio Taxis 163 Gilmore
Pl *031-229 5221*

City Cabs 2 Atholl Pl *031-228 1211*

Handicabs (Lothian) Ltd 14
Braefoot Terr *031-666 0955*

Radiocabs 5 Upper Bow *031-225 9000, 031-225 6736*

BRITISH RAIL

Approximate train journey times to
destinations within Scotland
Edinburgh—Glasgow   45 mins
Edinburgh—Inverness   4 hours
Edinburgh—Aberdeen   2½ hours
For information on fares and
services contact:

British Rail Waverley Station *031-556 2451*

Useful information

AUTOMOBILE ASSOCIATION

AA Centre 18–22 Melville St
Insurance Services *031-226 4031*
Travel Agency *031-225 3301*

BANKS

Allied Irish Banks 131 George St
031-226 5206
Open Mon–Fri 9.30–3.30
Bank of America 24 St Andrew
Sq *031-556 5561*
Bank of Credit and Commerce
3 St Andrew Sq *031-557 2720*
Bank of Nova Scotia 6 South
Charlotte St *031-226 3911*
Bank of Scotland The Mound *031-442 7777*
No charges made with National
Westminister, TSB, Co-op.
Open Mon–Wed & Fri 9.30–
4.45, Thu 9.30–3.30 & 4.30–
5.30
Barclays Bank 35 St Andrew Sq
031-557 2733
Foreign section available. Cash
point inside bank open 9.15–
4.45. Open Mon–Fri 9.30–3.30
British Linen Bank 4 Melville St
031-453 1919
Open Mon–Fri 9–5
Chemical Bank 17 Charlotte Sq
031-226 2987
Citibank Capital House, 2 Festival
Sq *031-228 3000*
Clydesdale Bank 29 George St
031-225 4081
Affiliated to the Midland Bank.
Foreign section available. TSB
Speedbank cards and Nat West
cards must be used at cash
points. Open Mon–Fri 9.30–
3.30, Thu also 4.30–6
Clydesdale Bank Edinburgh
Airport *031-333 3146*
Bureau de change facility. Open
Mon–Fri 8–7, Sat 9–4.30 (9–
2.30 in winter), Sun 11–5
Co-operative Bank 15/17 South St
Andrew St *031-557 3399*
Open Mon–Fri 9.30–3.30
County Bank 7 Forres St *031-226 6318*
Credit Lyonnais 86 George St
031-226 4324
First National Bank of Chicago
46 Charlotte Sq *031-226 5794*
**Hong Kong and Shanghai
Banking Corporation** Hobart
House, 76 Hanover St *031-225 9393*
Open Mon–Thu 9.30–12.30 &
1.30–3.30 (closes 4.30 Mon), Fri
9.30–3.30
Lloyds Bank 113/115 George St
031-226 4021
Foreign section available. Cash
points situated outside bank
Open Mon–Fri 9.30–3.30
Lombard North Central
20 Dublin St *031-557 3434*
National Girobank 93 George St
031-226 4301
Open Mon–Fri 9–5.30

National Westminster Bank
80 George St *031-226 6181*
Affiliated with Midland Bank
and Ulster Bank. Cash point
outside Bank (Midland cash
cards can be used)
Open Mon–Fri 9.30–3.30
Royal Bank of Scotland 42 St
Andrew Sq *031-556 8555*
Foreign section available. No
charges made with Bank of
Scotland and Nat West.
Open Mon–Fri 9.30–3.30, Thu
also 4.30–5.30
Société Générale 45 George St
031-225 7933
Standard Chartered Bank 18–20
George St *031-225 4615*
Open Mon–Thu 9.30–12.30 &
1.30–3.30, Fri 9.30–3.30
**Trustee Savings Bank of
Scotland** 28 Hanover St *031-226 3671*
Foreign section available

BUREAUX DE CHANGE

**Clydesdale Bank Bureau de
Change** Waverley Market *031-556 7306*
Open May & June Mon–Sat
8.30–7.30, Sun 11–3; Jul, Aug
& Sep Mon–Sat 8.30–8.30, Sun
11–3; Oct–end Apr Mon–Fri
9–5.30, Sat 9–12.30

EMERGENCIES

In life-threatening emergencies,
telephone 999 from any call-box
and say which service is required—
Fire Brigade, Police or Ambulance.
There is no charge for the call. See
also *Hospitals* and *Police Station*
below.

GUIDED TOUR SERVICES

WALKING TOURS
**The Cadies Scottish Personal
Guides,** 9 Belford Terr *031-332 3429*
**Countryside Ranger Service
Guided Walks** From the Visitor
Centre Hermitage of Braid. For
programme *031-447 7145*
Edinburgh Tours For details of
the Royal Mile Tour *031-661 0125*
Ghosts and Ghouls Two-hour
evening tour from the Mercat
Cross at 10pm
**Guided Walks around Historical
Cramond** Sunday tour Mr
Gibbs *031-336 6034*
Historical Edinburgh Tours
Evening tours (not during
Festival period) Miss
J Thompson *031-346 0212*
Mercat Tours Two-hour tour
from the Mercat Cross, High
Street at 2.30pm
New Town Walks Details of
daytime and evening walks from
New Town Conservation
Centre, 13a Dundas St *031-556 7054*

1868 City Tours Three-hour tours
of the Old Town in transport of
a bygone age
031-334 8211

CITY COACH TOURS

For details of coach tours of the
city contact:
Eastern Scottish, St Andrew
Square Bus Station *031-558 1616/7*
Lothian Region Transport,
Waverley Bridge *031-226 5087*
Scotline Tours, 87 High St *031-557 0162*

CHAUFFEUR-DRIVEN
GUIDED TOURS

Ghillie Personal Travel, 64
Silverknowes Rd East *031-336 3120*
Scottish Tours, 66 Cumberland St
031-556 0352
W L Sleigh Ltd, 99 Shandwick Pl
031-226 3080

HEALTH

CHEMIST
Boots the Chemist, 48 Shandwick
Pl *031-225 6757*
Open Mon–Sat 8am–9pm, Sun
11am–4.30pm

EMERGENCY DENTAL
SERVICE
**Accident and Emergency
Department,** Western General
Hospital, Crewe Rd South *031-332 2525*
Emergency service is available
7.30pm–10.30pm daily. At other
times contact the **Edinburgh
Dental Hospital,** 31 Chambers
St *031-225 9511* or the General
Dental Practitioner Services

HOSPITALS
24-hour accident and emergency
Royal Infirmary of Edinburgh,
1 Lauriston Place *031-229 2477*
Western General Hospital Crewe
Road South *031-332 2525*
For non-emergency medical
treatment contact the nearest
General Practitioner. Most hotels
and guesthouses will have a list of
addresses.

LIBRARIES

Central Library, George IV
Bridge *031-225 5584*
Fountainbridge Library,
137 Dundee St *031-229 4588*
McDonald Road Library
corner of McDonald Rd
and Leith Walk *031-556 5630*
Morningside Library,
184 Morningside Rd
031-447 1180
National Library of Scotland,
George IV Bridge *031-226 4531*
Stockbridge Library, Hamilton Pl
031-332 2173

NEWSAGENTS

International Newsagents,
367 High St *031-225 4827*
John Menzies, 107 Princes St, G2
10b Queensferry St, G2
31 Holm St, Tolcross
197 Whitehouse Rd, G4
6 Bridge Rd, G13
26 Elm Row, G7
65 St James Centre, G1

NEWSPAPERS

Morning daily
Daily Record
Glasgow Herald
Scottish Daily Express
The Scotsman
Evening daily
Evening News
Weekly
Scottish Sunday Express
Sunday Mail
Sunday Post

PHOTOGRAPHY

Magic Moments, 151 Gilmore Pl
031-229 7217
Same-day developing
Photo Lab Express, 103 Princes
St *031-225 1468*
24-hr developing

POLICE STATION

**Lothian & Borders Police
Headquarters,** Fettes Ave *031-
311 3131*
(includes lost property)

POST OFFICES

Edinburgh Head Post Office, 2–
4 Waterloo Pl, Edinburgh
EH1 1AA *031-550 8200*
Boroughmuirhead P O, 1
Merchiston Pl, Edinburgh
EH10 4NP *031-229 2857*
Forrest Road P O, 33 Forrest Rd,
Edinburgh EH1 2QP *031-
225 3957*
Frederick Street P O, 40
Frederick St, Edinburgh
EH2 1EY *031-226 6937*
Hope Street P O, 7 Hope St,
Edinburgh EH2 4EN *031-
225 7433*
Leith Walk P O, 263a Leith Walk,
Edinburgh EH6 8NY *031-
554 2988*
Newington P O, 41 South Clerk
St, Edinburgh EH8 9NZ *031-
667 1154*
Tollcross P O, 5 Brougham St,
Edinburgh EH3 9JS *031-229 8536*
Tyncastle P O, 66 Gorgie Rd,
Edinburgh EH11 2NB *031-
337 3673*

TV AND RADIO

TELEVISION STATIONS
BBC Television
Scottish Television
Channel Four
RADIO
BBC Radio Services Radio
Scotland 370m 810kHz
92.5–94.6 MHz
IBA Radio Services Radio Forth
194m 1548kHz 97.3 MHz

TOILETS

The following toilets, situated in
the city centre, are open 9am–6pm
and have facilities for the disabled.
Canongate (foot of the Royal
Mile)
Castle Terrace Car Park
Haymarket
The Mound Princes St
Ross Open-Air Theatre Princes
St Gardens (open May–Sep)
Waverley Market Princes St (open
24hrs)

TOURISM INFORMATION
CENTRES

Edinburgh Festival Fringe,
170 High St, EH1 1QS *031-
226 5257*
Edinburgh Festival Society,
21 Market St, EH1 1BW *031-
226 4001*
**Edinburgh Internationl Jazz
Festival,** 116 Canongate,
EH8 8DD *031-557 1642*
Edinburgh Military Tattoo, The
Tattoo Office, 22 Market St,
EH1 1QB *031-225 1188*
The National Trust for Scotland,
5 Charlotte Sq, EH2 4DU *031-
226 5922*
**Scottish Arts Council Arts
Information Centre,**
19 Charlotte Sq, EH2 4DF *031-
226 6051*
Open Mon–Thu 9–5.30, Fri
9–5. Information on concerts,
exhibitions, festivals, dance and
drama etc. in Edinburgh and
elsewhere in Scotland
**Scottish Development
Department,** Historic Buildings
and Monuments Division,
20 Brandon St *031-556 8400*
Scottish Tourist Board,
23 Ravelston Terr, EH4 3TP
031-332 2433
No personal callers
Scottish Travel Centre, South St
Andrews St *031-332 2433*
**Tourist Information and
Accommodation Centre,**
Waverley Market, Princes St,
EH2 2QP *031-557 2727*
Tourist Information Centre,
Edinburgh Airport *031-333 2167*

ANNUAL EVENTS

February	**International Rugby** at Murrayfield
March	**International Rugby** at Murrayfield
April	**Edinburgh Folk Festival**
June	**Royal Highland and Agricultural Show** Ingliston
August	**Edinburgh Book Festival**
	Edinburgh Festival Fringe
	Edinburgh Film Festival
	Edinburgh International Festival
	Edinburgh Jazz Festival
	Edinburgh Military Tattoo

INDEX

Page numbers in **bold** indicate main entries

Acknowledgements

The publishers would like to thank the Scottish Tourist Board and the City of Edinburgh District Council for their help in the preparation of this book.

Douglas Corrance was especially commissioned by The Automobile Association for this publication. All the photographs except those listed below were taken by him.

The AA also wishes to thank the following libraries and organisations for their assistance:

Reproduced by Gracious Permission of Her Majesty the Queen 51 The Morning Drawing Room Palace of Holyrood; *By Courtesy of Edinburgh City Libraries* 10 Early map of Edinburgh; *Edinburgh Festival Society* 27 Festival logo; *The Mansell Collection* 11 James Hepburn, 12 Prince Charles Edward Stuart, 14/15 View of the City, 30 George Heriot, 31 Drinking cup, 34 Robert Louis Stevenson, James Simpson, 41 Duddingston Loch; *Mary Evans Picture Library* 10 James IV, 33 William Burke, 33/34 Sir Walter Scott, 52 Harry Lauder; *National Galleries of Scotland* 11 Mary, Queen of Scots, Detail from portrait of Lord Darnley; *Royal Botanic Gardens* 32 Sir Robert Sibbald